Berlitz

Budapest

Original Text: Paul Murphy
Updater: Chris Lacey
Managing Editor: Clare Peel
Series Editor: Tony Halliday

D0424553

Berlitz® POCKET GUIDE

Budapest

Thirteenth Edition (2005)
Updated 2006
Reprinted 2006

PHOTOGRAPHY
Mark Read/Apa 11, 17, 22, 25, 27, 30, 31, 34, 40, 41, 47, 48, 51, 52, 55, 57, 58, 59, 64, 68, 70/1, 74, 94, 101, 102, 104; Neil Schlecht/Apa 15, 20, 32, 33, 37, 38, 42, 44, 53, 56, 60, 62, 76, 84, 87, 96, 98; Byron Russell/Apa 14, 29, 66, 79, 81, 82, 89, 92; Beryl Dhanjal 18, 65, 73; Berlitz 24, 91; Paul Murphy/Apa 13; Marton Radkai 6; Corbis/Edward Holub 8.
Cover photograph: Marcus Brooke

CONTACTING THE EDITORS
Every effort has been made to provide accurate information in this publication, but changes are inevitable. The publisher cannot be responsible for any resulting loss, inconvenience or injury. We would appreciate it if readers would call our attention to any errors or outdated information by contacting Berlitz Publishing, PO Box 7910, London SE1 1WE, England.
Fax: (44) 20 7403 0290;
e-mail: berlitz@apaguide.co.uk
www.berlitzpublishing.com

Mátyás Church (page 29) towers above the historic district

Museum of Fine Arts (page 67) has the city's best-regarded collection

Chain Bridge (page 47) and the Danube, which cuts the city in two

See massive figures from the Soviet era at the Statue Park (page 76)

TOP TEN ATTRACTIONS

Many of the buildings in the Old Town (page 32) have colourful façades

The Royal Palace (page 26), home to the Hungarian National Gallery, is splendid by day or night

The Parliament Building (page 59) with the statue of former Prime Minister Imre Nagy outside

City Park (page 68) is home to the zoo, with its iconic art nouveau elephant house

The Fishermen's Bastion (page 31) looks like a fairy-tale castle and is a popular spot for photographs

Gellért Hotel and Baths (page 40), for a taste of old-fashioned opulence

CONTENTS

A ➤ in the text denotes a highly recommended sight

Fact Sheets

INTRODUCTION

'*Budapest seems a wonderful place...the impression I had was that we were leaving the West and entering the East. The most western of splendid bridges over the Danube, which is here of noble width and depth, took us among the traditions of Turkish rule.*'

The opening lines of Bram Stoker's *Dracula* (1897) convey author Jonathan Harker's sense of entering truly unknown territory when he reached Budapest on his journey to Transylvania. In his day, Budapest was considered the limits of the civilised world – exotic, but rather frightening. Many thing have changed since then, and Hungary is now very much part of Europe – and officially so since it became a member of the European Union (EU) in May 2004. Its capital, Budapest, is a busy, increasingly cosmopolitan city with a growing tourist trade. New routes opened up by budget airlines ensure that Budapest is more accessible than ever before, yet, for the moment at least, it still retains much of its old-world charm.

Geography

Budapest is a city of two distinct parts, divided by the Danube, which, despite the waltz written in its honour, is murky and definitely not blue. The river separates the medieval streets and Roman

King Stephen stands guard at the Fishermen's Bastion

In AD1036, the wise King Stephen wrote to his son, Emeric: 'Make the strangers welcome in this land, let them keep their languages and customs, for weak and fragile is the realm which is based on a single language and culture.'

remains of Buda and Óbuda (meaning Old Buda) from the late-19th-century boulevards of Pest. On the west bank, in Buda, the hills rise above the river. Over a period of 800 years, Castle Hill has suffered 31 sieges and been reduced to rubble on numerous occasions, yet enough has survived for it to remain one of Europe's most appealing medieval enclaves. On the flat ground of the opposite bank lies Pest, a busy city with broad, leafy boulevards and handsome baroque, neoclassical and art nouveau buildings. Only in 1873 were these distinct areas merged to form one city.

Contemporary Budapest and its People

There's a lot more to the city than the historic sites and thermal baths for which it is famous. Since the end of the Soviet period Budapest has become very much a consumer city, with more than 20 modern shopping centres, numerous

Contemporary style in an historic street

hypermarkets and fast-food outlets. Many Budapestis wear fashionable clothes, drive decent cars – there's a feeling that the few old 'Trabis' are maintained from a sense of irony, not poverty – and have mobile phones. Hungarians are renowned for their friendliness. If they speak English (many of

> **Until World War II Budapest was known for its coffee houses, opulent places where the bourgeoisie and the intelligentsia congregated. Sadly, most have gone, but a few gems remain, joined now by modern counterparts** (*see Where to Go chapter for details*).

them, particularly the younger generation, are fluent in English or German) and they see you looking at a map, they will often volunteer help. If they don't speak English, they'll try their best to help – confronted with a foreigner who has got lost, missed a bus stop or can't understand the transport ticket machine, they will often take it upon themselves to help sort out the situation.

Eminent Hungarians

Hungary has produced some great musicians, such as Franz Liszt (1811–86), who became president of the Budapest Academy of Music. His disciple, Béla Bartók (1881–1945) later became a professor at the academy and collaborated with Zoltán Kodály (1882–1967) in collecting and publishing Hungarian folk songs. Writers include poet Sándor Petőfi (1823–49), who became a hero of the European revolutions of 1848, and Arthur Koestler (1905–83). George Soros, businessman and philanthropist, was born in Budapest, as was conductor Sir Georg Solti, who is also buried here. Seventeen Hungarians have won Nobel Prizes: holography was developed by prize-winning physicist Dennis Gabor, and Zsigmondy crater on the moon is named after Nobel laureate Richard Zsigmondy, who won the prize for chemistry in 1925.

Hollywood in its heyday was full of Hungarian talent, including a number of the great producers and directors – Korda, Fox, Zukor – and the revered Michael Curtiz who directed *Casablanca*. Actors include Béla Lugosi (best known for his role in the 1931 film *Dracula*) and the wonderfully sinister Peter Lorre. More recently, director István Szabó became internationally known and won an Oscar for *Mephisto* (1981).

Hungarians' contribution to the modern world is considerable. What would we do without the ball-point pen invented by László Biro? Tribute is also due to Béla Barényi, whose design produced the VW Beetle; and to Egon Ronay for the vast improvement in Britain's cooking. And the frustrating cube designed by Ernő Rubik in the mid-1970s was a huge succcess, and the forerunner of numerous other puzzles.

City Attractions

Budapest has a lot to offer. First, it's a spa city, so you can experience bathing, health and beauty treatments, new-age therapies and much more in wonderfully decadent surround-

A Lasting Impression

'Good men must die, but death cannot kill their names,' says an old proverb. In Budapest, many of the streets are named after Hungarian heroes. Some are historical figures, others belong to the more recent past. The writer George Mikes (who wrote *How to be an Alien*, a celebrated satirical book about England) returned to Budapest and found that his former friends had become 'streets, statues and boulevards...with a largish square, you once had a drunken fight at 3am in City Park. And that statue there – so majestic on his pedestal – used to go to bed with one of your girl friends. It hurt very much at the time – it was certainly not the behaviour you expect from a statue.'

The stunning view from the Gellért Hill

ings. It is also a city of culture. The banks of the Danube, the Castle district of Buda, and Andrássy út and the surrounding historical area are UNESCO World Heritage Sites. It has some excellent museums and galleries and is a city in which 'high culture' is within the reach of everyone. Hungarian cuisine has made great advances lately and a new generation of chefs in Budapest are producing innovative dishes, often based on traditional recipes adapted for 21st-century tastes.

Getting around Budapest is easy, either on foot or by the highly efficient public transport system *(see page 124)*.

Areas of natural beauty such as the Buda Hills are easily accessible from Budapest, as are the towns and villages along the scenic Danube Bend. You could also visit Lake Balaton, the nearest thing to the seaside this far inland, or the Puszta, the great plain, with its renowned horsemen. However, you may find so much to do in the city itself that these excursions will have to be saved for another occasion.

A BRIEF HISTORY

The Carpathian and Danube basins have been inhabited since around 350,000BC, according to archaeological evidence – fragments of bone and pottery – some of which can be seen in the National Museum in Budapest. However, the first identified occupants were a Celtic-Illyrian tribe, the Eraviscans, refugees from wars in Greece, who settled in the area of today's Budapest in the 3rd century BC. They established a tribal capital on top of Gellért Hill and a settlement in Óbuda. Some people believe they called the Óbuda settlement Ak Ink (meaning Ample Water), which accounts for the later Roman name, Aquincum. Others believe the Roman name comes from *aqua*, the Latin for water and *quinque* meaning five. Either way, it demonstrates the importance of water when the settlement was founded.

Enter the Romans

In the 1st century AD, Roman legions advanced to the Danube. By the second century, 20,000 Roman troops had been deployed along the river between Vienna and Budapest. The Romans built a military camp called Aquincum to command and coordinate this long frontier. Aquincum became home to 6,000 soldiers, and civilian suburbs housing up to 10 times that number of people grew from it. In AD106 Aquincum was made the capital of the Roman province of Lower Pannonia. As the Roman Empire crumbled, the forces of Attila the Hun besieged and captured the settlement and established a

The Golden Bull was promulgated by King András II after his nobles grew tired of his profligate ways. It created the framework for the Diet, an annual meeting of noblemen.

town on the west side of the river, which they named after Attila's brother, Buda. When Attila died in AD453, the Avars overthrew the Huns and occupied the area until the 9th century.

Magyars Migrate

The Magyars date their arrival to AD890. Their origins are a mystery, although it is thought that they came from the area between the Volga River and the Urals. The name Magyar stuck for both the country (Magyarország in Hungarian) and the language. Related tribes are thought to have travelled northwest to modern Finland and Estonia. Their difficult and only distantly related tongues are classified by linguists as Finno-Ugric.

Portrait of the Magyars

The first military leader of the Magyars, Prince Árpád, founded a dynasty that lasted more than three centuries. Prince Géza, his great-grandson, embraced Christianity, and on Christmas Day 1000, Géza's son, István (Stephen) was crowned the first king of Hungary in Esztergom. King Stephen built churches and spread Christianity and was canonised as Szent István (St Stephen). A landmark of the nation's civilisation in these early days was the Golden Bull of 1222, spelling out the rights of nobles and commoners.

The area was invaded by Mongols, who overran the country in 1241–2. Whole towns and villages, including Buda and

King Mátyás, Heroes' Square

Pest, were devastated by an orgy of killing and destruction, followed by famine and epidemics. The Mongols retreated, however, and King Béla IV set about restoring the nation, wisely constructing the rebuilt town of Buda within strong, fortified walls.

Trade and Culture

The Árpád dynasty ended in 1301, and Károly Róbert (Charles Robert) claimed the crown. Although he was an Angevin (a member of the ruling family of Anjou in France), his paternal grandmother was the daughter of Stephen V and she aroused Károly's interest in Hungary when he was a boy. He had to fight for control and underwent three coronations by various factions, the final one with the traditional holy crown. A man of great ability, Károly ruled well. Originally he set up his court in Visegrád but soon decided to move it to Budapest. He was thwarted for five years but eventually gained access by subterfuge and executed recalcitrant officials. A palace was built, trade was stimulated, Buda became the capital and Pest a commercial centre with city walls. The modern Little Boulevard, Kiskörút, follows the line of the old walls.

Other kings followed but the next major figure was János Hunyadi, a Transylvanian and national hero in the mid-15th century. The Ottoman Turks had been threatening the country for some time, and Hunyadi led the resistance. The young Polish king, chosen to rule Hungary after the death of Albrecht of Habsburg, was slain in the battle of Varna in 1444; Hunyadi was entrusted with the regency. When Albrecht's son, Ladislaus V, was of age, Hunyadi resumed his fight. He led the Hungarian army to victory against the Ottomans at Nándorfehérvár (now Belgrade) in 1456. When Ladislaus V died without an heir, in 1458, János Hunyadi's son, Korvin Mátyás (Matthias Corvinus Hunyadi), was elected to the throne. For the next 32 years, Hungary enjoyed a golden age of intellectual and civic development. Under this enlightened king's rule, the city of Buda became the focus of the country's cultural rebirth, and Pest flourished as the hub of trade and industry. King Mátyás's newly built Royal Palace on Castle Hill was the talk of Europe.

In 1490, Mátyás also died without an heir. The Hungarian barons extended their power, and a council of 39 took control, but failed to deal with the threat presented by the growing power of the Ottoman Turks. In 1514, the barons armed

Originally founded in the 15th century, the magnificent Royal Palace still dominates the Buda skyline

40,000 peasants, who were led by an officer called György Dósza. However, when assembled at Pest, the peasants showed that they had ideas of their own, and rebelled against the barons. Their rebellion was unsuccessful and they were reduced to serfdom; Dósza was executed. The Turkish forces were now superior and there was no effective opposition. The king, Lajos (Louis) II, and much of his army, were killed at the battle of Mohács (in southern Hungary) in 1526, and Hungary disappeared from the map of Europe for the following four centuries.

Memorials to the Past

In Budapest you can stroll through history. The Kerepesi Cemetery was the original national place of burial and many who shaped the nation's events are buried there, including Ferenc Deák and Lajos Kossuth *(see page 18)* and the journalists, writers and bohemians who were the original habitues of the coffee houses. Nearby lie the ranks of middle-class families: the Gerbeauds, respected restaurateurs, for example; and chess grand masters, the days long gone since they opened with the Budapest gambit.

The communist regime discouraged religious burials, so in allowing such funerals, Farkasreti Cemetery came to the fore. The graves of Bartók, Kodály and Sir Georg Solti may be found here. Imre Makovecz designed the mortuary chapel; the interior is a simalcrum of the human body, in which the dead lie at the heart. The mausoleums and other works of art that mark the graves range from the beautiful to the kitsch.

Hungarian cemeteries are also a place to find wooden gravemarkers, beautifully worked but with no inscriptions, as the carved icons carry all of the important information about the deceased.

Remember, though, that thousands have no memorials: the revolutionaries of 1956, for example, were buried where they fell.

The Habsburg rulers of neighbouring Austria, fearful that Vienna would be the Ottoman Empire's next conquest, proclaimed themselves rulers of Hungary in order to create a buffer zone between themselves and the Turks. Hungary was dismembered, with a narrow strip going to the Habsburgs, Transylvania becoming a principality under the Sultan's authority, and central Hungary falling under direct Turkish rule. Turkish occupation lasted almost a century and a half, although it left behind little of note except the thermal baths.

Ferenc Deák's mausoleum, Kerepesi Cemetery

The Habsburgs

In 1686–7, the Holy Alliance (comprising the Habsburgs, Poland and Venice) liberated Buda. However, there were Hungarians who wanted independence, not Habsburg rule. From 1703–11, Prince Ferenc Rákóczi (a descendant of the princes of Transylvania) led the struggle for independence. What began as a peasant uprising turned into a battle for liberation, but the country was too ravaged by war and poverty to sustain a rebellion.

Peace lasted for the rest of the 18th century, during which the country made great economic strides as a province of the Habsburg Empire. Pest expanded its role in international trade while Buda regained its status as Hungary's administrative hub. There was a period of reform when Hungarians like Count István Széchenyi secured development and economic reforms, while Lajos Kossuth sought social changes. In 1847, these two men, with Ferenc Deák and Count Lajos Batthyány, formed a liberal opposition party.

In 1848, a group of young intellectuals, including the 25-year-old radical poet, Sándor Petőfi, led a rebellion. They formed a short-lived provisional government, headed by Kossuth. The Emperor Franz Josef I summoned help from the Tsar of Russia, and crushed the revolt the following year.

Something had to be done, and the solution was proposed by Deák. The Compromise of 1867 turned Franz Josef's Austrian Empire into the altogether more grand Austro-Hungarian Empire. His wife Erzsébet (Elizabeth), popularly known as Sissi, was known to have been helpful and sympathetic to the Hungarian cause. Franz Josef and Erzsébet were crowned as rulers, and Count Gulya Andrássy was chosen to be prime minister.

The city's coat-of-arms

Rapid Growth

In the period from the Compromise to World War I Budapest grew faster than any other city in Europe. Industry, banking and commerce ensured economic growth, and grand buildings mushroomed across the city.

Count Széchenyi, who was a powerful force in the development of the city, is credited with responsibility for the Chain Bridge, which was the first such structure to span the Danube. It is said that his motivation was frustration when he had to wait a week to get across the river by boat to bury his father. It

> **Lajos Kossuth (1802–94)** became a popular hero throughout Europe in the 1840s. He was a fervent nationalist and under his influence Magyar replaced Latin as the language for laws, education and government business.

was Széchenyi who had the notion of uniting the towns of Buda, Óbuda and Pest into one city, and in 1873 Budapest was born.

In 1896 1,000 years of Magyar life in Hungary were celebrated. Hősök tere (Heroes' Square), the Országház (Houses of Parliament), Vajdahunyad Castle, the metro system under Andrássy út, the Opera House and much more all date from this heady time. The wealth of the city meant the blossoming of fashionable confectioners, shops and entertainment venues. Tourists arrived to 'take the cure' in the waters of Budapest's spas. Along with the cure, they also took coffee and pastries, just as visitors do today, at Ruszwurm, Gerbeaud, Lukács, Café Művész, the Centrál Kávéház and the New York Kávéház.

The Early 20th Century

In 1900, Budapest was Europe's fastest-growing city, but within a mere two decades it had been pushed back to its former status as a nondescript town of peripheral importance. World War I brought the good times to an end. Austro-Hungary was defeated, and the empire collapsed. An independent republic was set up under Count Mihály Károlyi. He resigned in March 1919 and a Communist Party, led by Béla

Kun, established a Soviet Republic. However, this was brought down shortly afterwards, in July, when the country was occupied and looted by Romanian forces.

In 1920 Admiral Miklós Horthy was proclaimed regent. The country was a monarchy once again, although it was decided not to recall the king. It was a most unusual situation – a powerful admiral in a landlocked country, appointed regent of a monarchy without a king.

Symbol of Soviet power at the Statue Park, near Budapest

World War II

An uneasy alliance with Germany existed throughout World War II, ending in March 1944 when German troops occupied Hungary. However, the Soviet Army was advancing fast. The Germans were defeated after a 14-week siege, and Budapest fell in February 1945. By the time the Russians assumed control of Budapest, three-quarters of its buildings had been demolished and the Hungarian death toll had reached half a million.

Soviet Rule

In 1949, Hungary was transformed into a People's Republic under Soviet rule. Forced public displays of loyalty could not disguise the fact that living standards were low and dissatisfaction was high. Stalinist leader, Mátyás Rákosi, established the sinister AVO secret police to ensure compliance with party doctrine by rooting out 'class enemies'.

After eight years of brutal repression, 50,000 students and workers marched on parliament to air their grievances on 23 October 1956. Angry students toppled a giant statue of Stalin near Heroes' Square, and the police fired on protesters outside the Hungarian Radio headquarters. The protest snowballed into a potent popular uprising that drew worldwide attention. Within days, a provisional Hungarian Government, led by the reformer Imre Nagy, had withdrawn Hungary from the Warsaw Pact. Soviet retribution took just 12 days. On 4 November, Red Army tanks rolled into Budapest and quickly crushed the resistance. The West watched in horror as Nagy and thousands more were executed. Some 25,000 Hungarians died and 200,000 fled the country.

The Soviets installed János Kádár as the new party boss. Although his rule began with repression, Kádár introduced some reforms, and in 1968 the New Economic Mechanism allowed a limited form of consumerism, known as 'goulash socialism'. In 1988–89, with the effects of *glasnost* and *perestroika* being felt throughout the Eastern bloc, Hungary experienced many changes. Restrictions of foreign travel were lifted and demonstrations prompted the Central Committee of the Communist Party to allow free elections in a multi-party system. The party then renounced Marxism and voted for its own dissolution. The People's Republic was terminated, and the Republic of Hungary was proclaimed.

> **The revolution of 1956 came about because Hungarians took all too literally Soviet leader Khrushchev's new doctrine of 'different roads to socialism'. The ferocity with which the Soviets destroyed the revolution – and the Hungarian Government – showed that no such roads were open.**

Hungary tore a gaping hole in the Iron Curtain by dismantling the barbed-wire barrier along the Austrian border, allowing access to the West. In 1990 the country held its first free elections in 43 years and again became a democratic republic, with a conservative government in power. In 1991 the last Soviet soldier left, and Hungary became an associate member of the European Union (EU); in 1994 a reformed socialist party came to power and in 1999 Hungary joined NATO.

Into the EU

On 1 May 2004 there were fireworks, celebrations and flag-waving as Hungary became a fully fledged member of the EU, following a vote the previous year. The then Prime Minister Péter Medgyessy said 'We can't expect Europe to offer a miracle. The miracle isn't within Europe. The miracle is within us. Europe is a wonderful change, a golden opportunity, but no more, and no less.' Earlier, Medgyessy and the Austrian Prime Minister Wolfgang Schüssel, had inaugurated a symbolic border station at Sopron-puszta, at the site where the Hungarians had allowed East Germans to cross to the West in 1989. Medgyessy said on that occasion 'Never again will any border on this site separate people from one another.'

Soldiers on Heroes' Square

Historical Landmarks

1st century AD Roman legions advance to the Danube.

890 The Magyars arrive in the area.

1000 Coronation of King (later St) Stephen.

1222 Proclamation of the Golden Bull, Hungary's Magna Carta.

1241–2 Mongol invasion destroys villages; famine and epidemics rife.

1301 Foundation of the Angevin dynasty by Károly Róbert.

1444 János Hunyadi chosen as regent

1456 Hunyadi's victory against the Ottomans at battle of Nándorfehérvár.

1458–90 Rule of Mátyás Corvinus Hunyadi.

1526 Battle of Móhacs leads to the division of Hungary and Ottoman rule.

1686–7 Liberation of Budapest by the Holy Alliance.

1703–11 Unsuccessful independence struggle, led by Ferenc Rákóczi.

1848–9 Rebellion of intellectuals, led by Sándor Petőfi.

1867 Foundation of the Austro-Hungarian Empire.

1873 Budapest formed from Buda, Pest and Óbuda.

1896 Celebrations to commemorate 1,000 years of Magyar life in Hungary.

1920 Miklós Horthy proclaimed regent.

1944 Hungary falls to German forces.

1945 Soviet Army defeats Germans; repressive Soviet rule ensues.

1956 The Hungarian revolution is brutally crushed by the Soviet Union. Party leader János Kádár is installed by Soviets but, surprisingly, is proved an agent for liberalisation, which begins slowly.

1958 Imre Nagy, prime minister at the time of the 1956 revolt, executed.

1988–9 Period of rapid change, as the Communist Party responds to public dissatisfaction. Soviet leader Mikhail Gorbachev promises no more interference in Hungarian affairs.

1989 Republic of Hungary proclaimed.

1990 Free elections return the Conservative Democratic Forum.

1991 Last Soviet soldier departs from Hungarian soil.

1999 Hungary joins NATO.

2004 Hungary joins the EU. Ferenc Gyurcsany becomes Prime Minister.

2006 Prime Minister Ferenc Gyurcsany's socialist-led coalition is re-elected.

WHERE TO GO

Getting around Budapest should not be a problem, as the majority of sights are clustered in the central areas. Castle Hill is tailor-made for walking, as are such inner-city boulevards as Andrássy út and the pedestrianised Váci utca. Most parts of town are served efficiently by the metro (subway), or by buses, trolley-buses, trams and the HÉV suburban railways.

For the most part, this section of the guide follows the natural layout of the city, starting on the western bank with Buda, Óbuda (Old Buda, just north of Buda) and the Buda Hills (further

Statues signifying the joining of Buda and Pest, Margaret Island

northwest), then crossing the Danube to Pest, on the eastern bank. We finally look at Margaret Island, which divides the Danube, excursions in the city suburbs and trips further afield.

BUDA'S CASTLE HILL AND OLD TOWN

The best place to begin a city tour is **Castle Hill** (Varhegy – *hegy* means hill), a steep limestone outcrop that rises some 50–60m (165–200ft) above the Danube. Castle Hill overlooks Pest from a long, narrow plateau divided into two sections. The southern part is occupied by the enormous former Royal Palace (where the original castle once stood, *see page 26*), while the northern district consists of the Vár, or Old Town.

Over the rooftops of Budapest, with Mátyás Church in the foreground

This part of Budapest has seen waves of destruction from invaders over the years, from Turks and Habsburgs to the Nazis and the Soviets, and many of its sites have been rebuilt more than once. Nowadays, however, the only invaders are tourists, who come to admire the picturesque, historic streets of an area that has been protected as a World Heritage Site since 1988.

There are various ways of getting up to Castle Hill. The most popular method is aboard the 19th-century funicular (*sikló*), which begins just beyond the end of the Chain Bridge and rises to the Royal Palace. As you approach the *sikló* terminus, notice the strange, oval-shaped structure beside the path: this is not a modern art installation, but the **kilometre stone**, from which all distances in Hungary are measured. On the wall beside the terminus, the national coat-of-arms is displayed, surrounded by those of the one-time provinces.

> You might notice that pigeons are somewhat less common in Budapest public squares than in other cities. It's rumoured that the city authorities have contraceptive pills ground up in the bird food.

If you don't want to use the funicular, there are alternatives, including minibuses that go up Castle Hill from Moszkva tér. From the metro, climb up the steps to the road and catch the very frequent Várbusz service that shuttles to and from Dísz tér, stopping at numerous points en route. You can also go up the hill on foot *(see page 28)*, but cars are not allowed unless you are staying at the Hilton.

The Royal Palace

The **Royal Palace** (Budavári palota), which dominates Castle Hill's southern skyline, is to the left as you emerge from the funicular. Begun in the 13th century as Buda Castle (Budai Vár), the palace reached its zenith in the 1400s under King Mátyás, when it was considered equal in grandeur to

The Royal Palace, illuminated at night

any in Europe. By the 16th century, sturdy ramparts had been erected for defence. The Turks took Buda by trickery, not by siege, but under the Ottoman Empire the palace fell into disrepair. The siege of 1686 saw it recaptured and placed under Habsburg rule, but the castle was almost wholly demolished, and the area became a backwater.

In the 18th century, the baroque town developed, and after the War of Hungarian Independence in 1849, the new Hungarian Government established its administrative centre in the castle district. Occupying German forces made the palace their headquarters during their final stand in 1945, causing immense damage. Since then, the palace has been rebuilt (mostly in the 1950s) to house some of Hungary's most important museums. In May 2004 it was announced that a further eight-year reconstruction programme on the castle was set to start, beginning with Mátyás Church, in the autumn of 2004.

If you are climbing Castle Hill, the best approach to the palace is from the steps at the southern tip of the hill beside the Medical History Museum *(see page 41)*. The path climbs through gardens to the rear entrance of the castle and the only surviving turreted tower, the **Buzogány** (Mace) Tower. Steps lead up through the tiny castle gardens to the entrance of the **Museum of Budapest History** (Budapesti Történeti Múzeum; open Mar–Oct Wed–Mon 10am–6pm; Nov–Feb 10am–4pm; admission charge) in Wing E of the Royal Palace. The museum displays the Gothic statues unearthed in 1974 and also covers the development of the city from the 5th century onwards.

Hungarian National Gallery

The palace and its collections are vast, and too extensive to see in a single day. Wings B, C and D house the **Hungarian National Gallery** (Magyar Nemzeti Galéria; open Tues–Sun 10am–6pm), which has splendid collections of medieval and Gothic art as well as popular exhibits of Hungarian Impressionism and 20th-century works (Wings C and D). Several rooms on the first floor are dedicated to Mihály Munkácsy, a 19th-century painter who became famous in Paris. His pictures are dark and gloomy in theme and became literally

---

The Ludwig Collection

Anybody interested in contemporary art should head for the Ludwig Collection (open Tues–Sun 10am–6pm; admission charge) in Wing A of the Hungarian National Gallery. Established in 1991 by Peter and Irene Ludwig, a German couple with collections in Aachen, Cologne and Vienna, it includes works by leading members of the American Pop Art movement – Andy Warhol, Roy Lichtenstein, Robert Rauschenberg and Claes Oldenburg. The Ludwigs also amassed a huge collection of works by Picasso, three of which are exhibited here.

more dark and gloomy as a result of the bitumen he mixed with his paint. Look out also for the works of Hungarian painters László Mednyánszky, József Rippl-Rónai and Károly Lotz, as well as János Vaszary's pivotal *Golden Age* and the odd but striking works of Tivadar Kosztka Csontváry, on the second-floor landing.

The southern palace courtyard includes Wing F, which houses the two million volumes of the **Széchenyi National Library** (Széchenyi könyvtár Bibliothek). The library is open to the public, and temporary exhibitions are held in the building.

Impressionist art in the Hungarian National Gallery

Mátyás Church

The **Old Town** essentially consists of four parallel streets, packed with colourful houses, historic monuments and small museums. A short walk to the right of the funicular terminus brings you to Dísz tér (Parade Square), which marks the start of the northern section of Castle Hill.

The 80-m (260-ft) spire of **Mátyás (or Matthias) Church** (Mátyás templom; church and museum open Mon–Fri 9am–5pm, Sat 9am–1pm, Sun 1pm–5pm; admission charge) towers gracefully over the historic district. Otherwise known as the Church of our Lady, the building is called Mátyás Church because there is a coat-of-arms of Mátyás Corvinus

Hunyadi (1458–90) on the tower. The crow that can be seen above the church is a reference to Mátyás, whose nickname 'Corvinus' came from the symbol on this coat-of-arms (*corvinus* = crow). He was Hungary's most popular medieval king and was married here (twice) in the 15th century. The Habsburg Emperor Franz Josef I was crowned King of Hungary here in 1867, to the tune of the *Coronation Mass,* composed for the occasion by Franz Liszt (1811–86).

The original church was built in the mid-13th century, converted into a mosque during the Turkish occupation, and seriously damaged during the reconquest of Buda in 1686. It was rebuilt in baroque style after the return of the Christian forces, and between 1873 and 1896 it was completely reconstructed along its present neo-Gothic lines. The unusual diamond-patterned roof, the geometric designs on the interior walls and the stained-glass windows and frescoes date from refurbishment in the 19th century.

Looking towards the romantic Fishermen's Bastion

In the **Loreto Chapel**, immediately to the left of the entrance, stands a treasured red-marble statue of the Virgin. A staircase, entered on the left-hand side of the church, leads to the entrance to the crypt and to the **Collection of Ecclesiastical Art**. The museum rambles up and down various old staircases, offering an excellent view, at one point, down onto the nave. There is a fine collection of medieval stone carvings, historic vestments, religious paintings, and relics, including a replica of the **Crown of St Stephen**.

In Trinity Square (Szentháromság tér) in front of the church is the **Holy Trinity Column**, crowded with statues of saints and angels. It

Fountain on Castle Hill

was erected in 1713 by grateful survivors of a plague epidemic. Across the square, towards Dísz tér, the white, two-storey baroque building with a jutting corner balcony served as Buda's town hall from 1710 to 1873.

Along the adjacent **Szentháromság utca** (the street that joins the four parallel streets alongside Mátyás Church) notice the medieval barrel-vaulted doorways on your way to No. 7, the **Ruszwurm** confectionery shop. One of the most prestigious in Europe, it was founded in 1827 and is still going strong. Nothing has changed: the cosy Biedermeyer-style furnishings have survived all the vicissitudes of the past two centuries, and the cakes and pastries are irresistible.

Fishermen's Bastion

Directly behind Mátyás Church is one of the most photographed edifices in Budapest, the intriguingly named **Fishermen's Bastion** (Halászbástya), built onto the castle walls. At first glance, this romantic array of turrets, terraces and arches resembles a fairy-tale castle and could pass for a medieval fortification. In fact, it was constructed around the turn of the 20th century purely for ornamental reasons. The

Elaborate art nouveau cafe sign

monument's name is a reference to the fishermen who defended the ramparts here in the 18th century. Today bus-loads of tourists photograph each other beneath the arches, the backdrop being one of the city's finest views, across the Danube and over to the Houses of Parliament. If you want to walk around the top of the walls you will have to pay (summer months only), but the views down below are similar and free. Nearby is the handsome equestrian statue of King Stephen (István), the first king of Hungary, who was canonised in 1083. Old ladies trade Transylvanian tablecloths here, and street musicians often fill the air with the sounds of Bartók and Liszt.

Just west of the Fishermen's Bastion is the jarring façade of the mirrored, six-storey Budapest Hilton Hotel. The bold approach of merging ancient and modern has integrated this 1977 Hilton Hotel with the remains of a 17th-century Jesuit college and the tower of a 13th-century Dominican monastery, and the result is not to everyone's liking. Across Hess András tér, the bas-relief on the **Red Hedgehog** at No. 3 is the sign from the building's days as an inn during the 18th century. No. 4 is the place where the first book in Hungarian was printed in 1473, by András Hess.

Touring the Old Town

Begin your tour of the district's old streets along delightful **Táncsics Mihály utca**. At No. 7, where Beethoven stayed in 1800, is the **Music History Museum** (closed for refurbish-

ment until summer 2006; open Mar–Dec Tues–Sun 10am–
6pm; admission charge), where you will find orchestral
instruments from Haydn's day and information on Bartók's
career. You will discover that bagpipes originated in Hungary. Next door, at No. 9, are plaques to the political heroes
Mihály Táncsics and **Lajos Kossuth**, both imprisoned here
in the 1830s and 1840s for their nationalist beliefs. No. 26
served as a synagogue from the late 14th century and has a
small museum relating to this period. The street ends at the
Vienna Gate (Bécsi kapu), a reminder that the district was
once fully enclosed. The grand structure to the left of
the gate, with the diamond-patterned roof, echoing that of
Mátyás Church, houses the **National Archives**.

Around the corner is **Fortuna utca**, an attractive and much-
photographed street of pastel-painted houses. It takes its name
from a tavern that stood at No. 4, from 1785 to 1868. Today,

A colourful façade in Fortuna utca, in the Old Town

the former inn houses the **Museum of Commerce and Catering** (Kereskedelmi és Vendéglátóipari Múzeum; open Wed–Fri 10am–5pm, Sat–Sun 10am–6pm; admission charge), which is more interesting than it probably sounds. There are exhibits on confectionery in one section and on Hungarian trade during the late 19th–early 20th century in the other, and the museum curators take a genuine delight in demonstrating various exhibits.

At Szentháromság tér, turn back into **Országház utca**. *Országház* means Houses of Parliament, and the street takes its name from the parliamentary sessions that took place in the building at No. 28 between 1790 and 1807. The architectural highlights here include the grand 15th-century

Touring the traditional way

mansion, now occupied by the **Alabárdos** (Halbadier) restaurant, and Nos 18–22, which are considered among the finest examples of 14th- and 15th-century domestic architecture on the hill. Several other buildings incorporate picturesque medieval features, at times hidden just inside the arches. Here you will see ancient stone *sedilia* (built-in seats for three people) and strings of paprika strung out to dry across windows and balconies. Although the area is a magnet for visitors, many Budapestis still live here.

At the end of Országház utca rises the ruined **Church of Mary Magdalene**, converted to a mosque under the Turks and reduced to knee-high remains by the Allies in the last days of World War II. Amazingly, its huge 15th-century tower survived. One stone-traceried window was rebuilt, but the rest of the church was left in ruins as a poignant reminder of wartime destruction. A more light-hearted curiosity is visible on the corner of Országház utca and Petermann bíró utca, but you have to look up to see it. A 'flying nun' (a convent occupied No. 28 before the parliament) has apparently passed straight through the corner of the building. Miklós Melocco executed this whimsical sculpture in 1977.

Úri utca (Gentlemen's Street) is even more ancient than Országház utca, and the houses have some fascinating details. There's another specialist museum at No. 49: the **Telephone Museum** (Telefonia Múzeum; open Tues–Sun 10am–4pm; admission charge) proudly claims that in 1881, Budapest had the world's first telephone exchange.

No. 9 Úri utca is the entrance to the **Buda Castle Labyrinth** (Budavári Labirintus; open daily 9.30am–7.30pm; admission charge), a maze of tunnels, some of which are natural (created by hydro-thermal activity) and some man-made, and originally used as cellars and bomb shelters.

Úri utca terminates at Dísz tér, where it is best to turn and walk back along **Tárnok utca**. The **Aranyhordó** (Golden Barrel) restaurant stands out, with orange-and-red geometric frescoes painted on the overhanging first floor. Next door, No. 18, was built as a merchant's house in the first half of the 15th century. From 1750 until 1913, it was the **Golden Eagle Pharmacy** (Arany Sas patikaház; open Tues–Sun 10am–6pm; free). Today it is the most attractive and idiosyncratic of the district's small museums, the Pharmacy Museum (Patika Múzeum). Beautiful old majolica vessels join informative displays on the potions and alchemical practices deployed in Budapest. Ask one of the guides to point out such curiosities as the 2,000-year-old mummified head that was used to provide the 'mummy-head dust' prescribed for treating bronchitis.

The last street in this district is leafy **Tóth Árpád sétány**. This promenade, which runs along the western ramparts, offers views of the Buda Hills, the huge southern railway station (Déli pályaudvar) and the green space called **Vérmező Park**. Vérmező means 'the field of blood', a name commemorating the execution site, in 1795, of a number of Hungarian Jacobins, who were considered dangerous as they disseminated the ideas of the Enlightenment and opposed the monarchy. Tóth Árpád sétany is the perfect place for a stroll, particularly in the early evening, when Budapestis come out to enjoy the fresh air. At the northern end, assorted cannons announce the entrance to the **Museum of Military History** (Hadtörténeti Múzeum; open Apr–Sept Tues–Sun 10am–6pm; Oct–Mar 10am– 4pm; admission charge). The extensive armaments exhibition is popular with children, and the section dedicated to the 1956 uprising *(see page 21)* is likely to make the most impact on older visitors.

BUDA RIVERSIDE

Viziváros (Watertown)

The district between Castle Hill and the Danube is called **Viziváros**, or **Watertown**. In the Middle Ages, the red-roofed district was where commoners lived, beyond the walled area for royalty and wealthier merchants on Castle Hill. During the Ottoman era, the Turks transformed the area's churches into mosques and constructed splendid public baths. Today the busy urban area is the site of new hotels, built here to capitalise on the proximity to Castle Hill and the unbeatable views of the sprawling Houses of Parliament opposite, across the river.

The section of riverside lying to the north of the Chain Bridge is an area of wonderful arcades and terraces, adorned with neoclassical statues and ceremonial staircases, as well as gateways (closed to the public) leading up to the Royal Palace. The area can be reached on foot from Castle Hill, or by taking the metro, bus, tram, or suburban railway to **Batthyány tér**, a major square and a city transport hub.

The Vienna stagecoach terminal was once just around the corner from Batthyány tér, and the famous **White Cross Inn**, on the side of the square opposite the river, was a fashionable venue for grand balls and other celebrations. It is still a majestic old building, even if its role has now been reduced to that of a nightclub, renamed Casanova after the Venetian libertine, who is reputed to have stayed here. On the south side of the square rise the twin towers of the fine, baroque **St Anne's Church** (Szent Anna templom; 1740–62), a fine structure with Italianate influences.

Király Baths, built by the Turks during the 16th century

Further north along **Fő utca** are the **Király Baths** (Király fürdő; open for men Tues, Thurs and Sat 9am–7pm; for women Mon, Wed and Fri 7am–5pm). In addition to the steam bath, visitors can use the sauna and other facilities. The name Király, which means king, was the family name of the early 19th-century owners of the baths. Established by the Turkish Pasha of Budapest in 1565, the authentic Turkish section has survived, complete with a large, octagonal pool under a dome.

Turn left off Frakel Leó út (the continuation of Fő utca) at Margit híd (Margaret Bridge) and follow signs up the steps to Mecset utca and another memento of Turkish times, the **Tomb of Gül Baba** (Gül Baba türbéje; open daily 10am–4pm; admission charge). Gül Baba was a whirling dervish, killed during the siege of Buda in 1541. Suleiman the Magnificent ordered the tomb to be built, and the Turkish Government have renovated the site. A statue of the great man stands just outside the shrine. There's a story, probably apocryphal, that Gül Baba brought the rose to Budapest. He is known as Father of the Roses, and the hill on which the mausoleum stands is called Rózsadomb (Hill of the Roses). It is now one of the most sought-after addresses in Budapest.

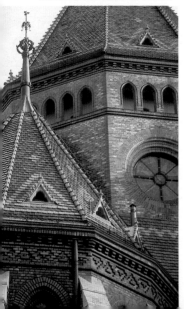

A patchwork of glazed tiles on the roof of the Calvinist Church

By contrast with the austerity of the mausoleum, the 1896 neo-Gothic **Calvinist Church** is recognised by its exuberant tile-and-brick exterior. It stands along the river towards the Chain Bridge, just to the south of Batthyány tér.

Gellért Hill

While Castle Hill provides arguably the finest views over the River Danube, another lookout point just to the south of the Royal Palace should not be missed. ► **Gellért Hill** (Gellérthegy), which rises some 140m (460ft) almost directly above the Danube on the Buda side, affords a wide panorama of the city.

Gellért was a Venetian missionary, Bishop Gerardus, who was martyred in the 11th century, by being put into a spike-studded barrel and thrown into the Danube. The place where this most foul of deeds was committed was marked in 1902 by the construction of a statue of Gellért, holding a cross, and it is still as if he is blessing city of Budapest.

The hill is not particularly well served by public transport, although there is a bus, No. 27, from Móricz Zsigmond Kör tér that goes most of the way. The climb, starting from the Gellért Hotel, is strenuous, and somewhat frustrating, as it often looks as if you are nearly there, but as you round the corner you find you still have a long way to go. There are, however, seats and views to compensate for your efforts, and as you climb, you may see flowers, birds and butterflies to admire – Hungary is reputed to have more butterflies than anywhere else in Europe. To the right as you set out, look out for the extraordinary and atmospheric Cave Church (open daily 8am–9pm), which belongs to the Order of St Paul, the only monastic body of Hungarian origin.

The **Citadel** (Citadella) crowning the hill was constructed by the Austrians after the Revolution of 1848 as a lookout point from which to control adjacent Castle Hill. Despised by Hungarians as a symbol of occupation, the Citadel saw no action, however, until the end of World War II, when German

The Liberation Monument

forces were trapped here and kept the city under fire until they surrendered. The Citadel has been renovated and now holds a restaurant and cafe, but it is most typically visited for the fine panoramic views.

The 40-m (132-ft) tall **Liberation Monument** (or Szabadság szobor), which is visible from all parts of the city, stands below the citadel. The Russians erected it in memory of their troops who fell fighting the Germans. The monument is loathed by the majority of local people as a symbol of Soviet domination, but it has become too much of a city landmark to remove, although some of its elements have now been relegated to the Statue Park *(see page 76)*.

At the base of the hill, the **Gellért Hotel and Baths** (Gellért Szálló és fürdő) is the perfect place to recover from your walk. Behind the classic, 1918 art nouveau structure is a huge, landscaped, outdoor swimming pool complex, while inside (entry on Kelenhegyi út 4) are the finest thermal baths in Buda (open 6am–6pm). The unisex indoor pool has a vaulted glass ceiling and Roman-style carved columns, while the thermal baths (segregated by sex) feature marble statues, fine mosaics and glazed tiles.

Although the Gellért reigns supreme among Budapest's thermal baths, there are two more historic baths *(fürdő)* along the Buda embankment, located near the Erzsébet híd (Elizabeth Bridge). The entrance to the male-only **Rudas fürdő** (pool open Mon–Fri 6am–6pm; thermal baths Mon–

Fri 6am–8pm; both Sat 6am–1pm) is at Döbrentei tér 9. The baths were opened in 1550, and although the building has been much altered over the centuries, the timeless atmosphere is authentic as ever in the steamy main pool, where a stone Turkish dome covers an octagonal pool, and sunlight streams in through the star-shaped glass openings in the grand cupola.

The 16th-century **Rác gyógyfürdő** on Hadnagy utca is undergoing reconstruction and should re-open in 2006. Legend has it that King Mátyás used to visit the baths, using secret tunnels connected to the Royal Palace.

The **Medical History Museum** (Semmelweis Orvostörténeti Múzeum) open Tues–Sun 10.30am–4pm; admission charge) on Apród utca 1–3, is named after Professor Semmelweis *(see page 45)*. Here you can learn about old-fashioned medical instruments and techniques, some of which appear worse than the conditions they were intended to relieve. There is also a beautifully preserved pharmacy, dating from 1813.

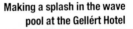

Making a splash in the wave pool at the Gellért Hotel

ÓBUDA

Óbuda – Old Buda – is the most ancient section of the city, being the site of the Roman city of Aquincum, built in the first century AD as the capital of the province of Lower Pannonia. The 'aqua' part of the name indicates the importance of building a settlement close to the water. Nowadays the area is scarred by heavy traffic using the main northern highway out of the city, and by cheaply constructed, Soviet-style residential buildings. It is in this unlikely setting that Hungary's most impressive Roman ruins are to be found.

➤ The civilian town of **Aquincum**, constructed for artisans, merchants, priests and other non-military staff, can be reached by HÉV train from Batthyány tér in 20 minutes. Just past the massive Auchan hypermarket the remains of a Roman aqueduct can be seen in the central carriageway of the motorway, running close to the railway.

The archaeological site covers a large area and comprises the foundations of villas, workshops and public areas. You will need a little imagination to recreate the scene as it was when

The impressive remains of the Roman city of Aquincum

40,000 people lived here nearly 2,000 years ago, but you will find help in the **Aquincum Museum** (Szentendrei út 139; open mid-Apr–Oct Tues–Sun 10am–5pm; admission charge) attached. Here the best of the finds are displayed, including tombstones, statues, mosaics and the remains of a water organ.

Returning towards Batthyány tér, more Roman ruins are located near Arpád hid (and near the bus terminal at Szentélek tér, if you want to catch a bus back). If you enter the subway beneath the Flórián tér overpass, you'll find assorted Roman remains and a singular sight – Roman baths, open to the sky, beneath the central reservation of the motorway. Take the subway exit on the opposite side from the baths to see another incongruous sight: a dozen isolated Corinthian columns set against the backdrop of a 1960s housing estate. The columns are on a grassy piece of parkland where local people walk their dogs. Some further ruins can be seen here and it's a good place to picnic.

The remains of the amphitheatre of the military town are further south on the corner of Pacsirtamező utca and Nagyszombat utca. Gladiators performed here in the 2nd century AD to entertain some 15,000 legionnaires.

There is more to Óbuda than its Roman heritage. Immediately north of Szentlélek tér is **Fő tér**, the old town square, which is small, picturesque and handsomely renovated. Open-air summer concerts are held in the square. The **Zichy Palace**, the handsome baroque building that dominates the square, is now the **Vasarely Museum** (open Tues–Sun 10am–5pm; admission charge). It features work by Victor Vasarely, the internationally renowned pioneer of the Op Art Movement, which exploits optical effects, characterised by cubes and spheres in brilliant colours.

Standing near the **Imre Varga Museum** (Laktanya utca 7; open Tues–Sun 10am–6pm; admission charge) are whimsical figures with umbrellas – a clue to the collection housed

A doorway on colourful Fő tér

inside. Varga is renowned as Hungary's greatest living sculptor, and whether his materials and subject matter are conventional, as in *Umbrellas*, or more offbeat, as with many of his other works, he always remains accessible and popular.

The other major museum in the area is the **Kiscelli** Kiscelli út (108; open Tues–Sun 10am–4pm; admission charge). It is best reached by taking tram No. 17 from Margaret Bridge to the terminal and then walking uphill towards the baroque mansion, once a Trinitarian monastery. The building now houses parts of the Budapest History Museum's collections of fine art and displays on modern urban history.

BUDA HILLS

The **Buda Hills** are a wooded area due west of Rózsadomb (the hill on which the tomb of Gül Baba stands), stretching as far north as Óbuda and as far south as the start of the M7 motorway. On a clear day, make the 15-minute walk or catch any one of the several trams or buses that go to the cog railway terminus, west of Moszkva tér (one of the city's major transport hubs) and opposite the Hotel Budapest.

The cog railway, which takes you up to **Széchenyi-hegy**, winds up through smart residential housing. At the terminus at the top there's a signpost pointing to **Gyermekvasút**, the Children's Railway (<www.gyermekvasut.com> for timetables). This is an 11-km (7-mile) narrow-gauge railway run by children, although adults drive the engines and the regulations of the MÁV state railways apply.

If you want to go up the hill when neither the Children's Railway nor the cog railway are operating (Sept–Apr; closed on Mon), take bus No. 21 which runs from Moszkva tér to **Normafa**, which functions as a ski resort when there's enough snow. From the bus terminus at Normafa, you can enjoy walking, running or cycling in the forest. **János-hegy** is an enjoyable walk of about 45 minutes (each way) through the woods, with plenty of fauna and flora to admire en route.

If you would like to return to town by a different route, there is a chairlift, **Zugliget** (closed some Mondays) that descends to a camp site, from where you catch the No. 158 bus back to Moszkva tér. As you float peacefully down the mountain-side, you will enjoy some spectacular views over forests to the spires and rooftops of the city.

Professor Semmelweis

Professor Semmelweis was born in Buda in 1815. While working in Vienna, he noticed that cases of puerperal fever were 13 percent among patients treated by doctors and only 2 percent among women treated by midwives. The death of a friend who had cut his finger while performing an autopsy and who died of symptoms similar to puerperal fever alerted Semmelweis to the fact that doctors did autopsies first thing in the morning, then went on to examine living patients. He had the idea that doctors should wash their hands in-between examinations. This notion was not well received at first, but the hand-washing achieved sweeping reductions to rates of infection. Despite this, Semmelweis suffered from the attitude of colleagues who thought him a charlatan. Eventually, he was admitted to an asylum and, it is said, died of infection caused by a cut to the hand.

At this point if you want to explore the hills further, there are several places of interest; most can be reached by bus or train. Take bus No. 5 to the home of **Béla Bartók**, now preserved as a memorial (Bartók Béla Emelékház; open Tues–Sun 10am–5pm; admission charge), at II Csalán utca 29. There are concerts on Friday evening in spring and autumn, and the Bartók String Quartet performs annually on 26 September, the anniversary of the composer's death.

Hármashatár-hegy (Three Border Hill) is another pleasant spot to relax, hike, picnic and enjoy views of the city. Sometimes, hang-gliding enthusiasts use it as a take-off point. It's reached by going to the terminal on bus No. 65.

The hills offer rare opportunities for speleology. Some caves are accessible to the public, including **Pálvölgyi barlang** (open Tues–Sun 10am–4pm; admission charge) on Szépvölgyi út. It is vast, with about 7km (4½ miles) explored so far. Some 500m (1,640ft) can be covered on guided tours; walking is not too difficult, but there is some ladder-climbing so you need suitable footwear. Nearby, on Pusztaseri út, is **Szemlő-hegyi barlang** (open Wed–Sun 10am–4pm; admission charge; guided tours available), which has incredibly beautiful mineral formations and stalactites and stalagmites.

CROSSING THE DANUBE

Returning now to the city centre, this section takes us down the Danube from north to south. The first bridge reached is the relatively modern **Árpád híd** (*híd* = bridge), which gives access to Margaret Island (Margitsziget, *see page 75*). At the southern end of the island is **Margaret Bridge** (Margit híd), which is really two bridges at an angle, with access to the island from the centre. It is the modern replacement of the 19th-century version destroyed in World War II and links the Grand Boulevard to Buda.

If Tower Bridge epitomises London, Brooklyn Bridge symbolises New York, and the Golden Gate is the pride of San Francisco, Budapest, too, has its landmark crossings.

The impressive **Chain Bridge** (Széchenyi Lánchíd), inaugurated in 1849, was the first bridge to link Buda and Pest, and one of its intial functions was to enable the Hungarian army of independence to flee from the advancing Austrians. Count István Széchenyi, a great innovator, imported the technology and expertise of Britain's industrial revolution to assist Hungary's own reform programme. An English engineer, William Tierney Clark, designed the Chain Bridge, and its construction was supervised by a Scotsman, Adam Clark (no relation), after whom the square at the Buda end of the bridge is named.

The bridge has graceful twin arches and is guarded by a pair of massive stone lions at each approach. Don't miss seeing

Taking to the river

the bridge when it is floodlit at night – it is one of the city's finest sights.

South of the Chain Bridge is the somewhat functional-looking **Elizabeth Bridge** (Erzsébet híd), named after the consort of Franz Josef. The original was destroyed during World War II and was replaced – this was less expensive than rebuilding the original – with a suspension bridge, which opened in 1964. The next bridge you reach is the green-ironwork **Liberty Bridge** (Szabadság híd), which was built for the 1896 millennium of the conquest of the Carpathian Basin and originally called the Franz Josef Bridge. Look for the turul birds perched on golden balls balancing on each pillar *(see page 78)*.

There are some interesting displays of the technology of the bridges at the Transport Museum (Közlekedési Múzeum) in Vidám Amusement Park *(see page 69)*.

Chain Bridge was the first such structure to link Buda and Pest

Further south are the functional, 1930s **Petőfi Bridge** and the newest bridge, **Lágymányosi híd**, completed in 1995. Crossing any of the bridges takes you to Pest, on the east side of the Danube.

The Pest riverside offers splendid views of Buda and the hills beyond, and one of the nicest things to do in Budapest is take tram No. 2,

At the grand opening of Széchenyi Lánchíd, the Chain Bridge, it is said that a small boy (rather like the boy in *The Emperor's New Clothes*) exclaimed loudly: 'The lions have no tongues!' So embarrassed was the designer, he jumped into the Danube and was never seen again.

which follows the river. Get off near Vigadó tér, where people like to stroll, meet friends and enjoy the cafe terraces. On the railings on **Dunakorzó** (the pedestrianised embankment), look out for the *Little Princess*, a statue of a quaint little girl with a jester's hat. She has shiny knees because people touch them for luck. Nearby is a statue of Shakespeare, which was unveiled on 23 April 2003 (exactly 439 years after he was born and 387 years after he died). This is a copy of an original statue by Andor Mészáros, which is in Ballarat, Australia.

PEST

Modern Budapest lies east of the Danube in what was, until 1873, the autonomous city of Pest. With its conglomeration of hotels, museum, government offices, banks, shopping streets, nightclubs, cafes, busy boulevards and handsome art nouveau apartment buildings, Pest is where the pulse of the modern capital beats strongest.

The Inner City (Belváros)

In AD294 the Romans built a fortress on the great expanse of flat plains to the east of the river to make it harder for invaders to establish a foothold near their garrison. They called the place Contra-Aquincum; today it is the core of the Inner City (Belváros), the shopping and entertainment centre of Budapest.

➤ The focal point of Pest's pedestrian zone is **Váci utca** (pronounced *Vah-tsee oot-sa*), where you can buy clothes, cosmetics, jewellery, art and books. You will also find lots of restaurants and cafes. Budapestis – joined by foreign visitors – parade up and down this street every evening.

Váci utca empties north into the shopping square called **Vörösmarty tér**, one of Pest's most popular gathering places. A classic rest stop for residents and visitors alike is **Gerbeaud**, doyen of Budapest's cafe scene since 1884. If the sumptuous, high-ceilinged interior is a little too formal for your liking, then take a terrace seat and watch the world go by.

Stroll a few yards towards the river and you will come to **Vigadó tér**, a pleasant riverside square with unequalled views of Castle Hill. Here, too, you will find craft stalls, and any number of buskers. A vibrant cafe-restaurant fills one side of the square, but the dominant building is the **Pesti Vigadó Theatre**. The acoustically perfect auditorium was renovated in 1980 (its predecessors having perished through war and revolution), but the glorious, mid-19th century Hungarian-Eastern style façade has survived. The list of performers and conductors who have graced the Vigadó Theatre is a Who's Who of the past 150 years of European classical music: Liszt, Brahms, Wagner, Mahler, Bartók, Prokofiev, Casals, Björling and von Karajan among them.

From Vörösmarty tér, take Deák Ferenc utca to busy Deák tér. This is the only point where all three metro lines meet, so it is an apt place for the tiny **Metro Museum** (Földalatti Vasúti Múzeum; open Tues–Sun 10am–5pm), located in a former station, in the Deák tér subway. Here you can see the train that travelled on Europe's first continental underground railway in 1896.

Also on Deák tér, at No. 4, is the **National Lutheran Museum** (Evangélikus Országos Múzeum; open Tues–Sun 10am–6pm; admission charge), charting the history of Protestantism in this largely Catholic country, and containing Martin Luther's will, dated 1542. Almost opposite is the **Tourinform** office *(see page 128)*. The mustard-coloured building dominating the far side of the square is the **Anker Palace**, formerly an insurance company headquarters and one of the few structures to escape World War II unscathed.

Walk down Barczy utca, which runs along the back of the Lutheran Church and, on your right, the **Budapest City Hall** fills an entire street. It was built in 1711 as a home for disabled soldiers, served for a time as an army barracks, and became the town hall in 1894. The 19th-century, neoclassical Pest County Hall lies a little further along the same street.

A seat on the terrace at the Gerbeaud Cafe

Nearby is Szervita tér, notable for a splendid art nouveau mosaic on the gable of the **Turkish Banking House** (Török Bánkház). Head south along Petőfi Sándor utca; on your right is the **Paris Arcade** (Párizsi Udvar), built in 1909, with exotic art nouveau details and a stained-glass ceiling.

Churches and University Buildings

Three fine churches and part of the university complex lie across the busy road (use the underpass). The **Franciscan Church** (Ferenciek templom), built in 1758, stands on the corner of Ferenciek tere. A relief on the side depicts the flood of 1838, which caused massive destruction to the inner city. Continue along Károlyi

Entering the Franciscan Church

Mihály utca, past the yellow University Library building on the left. On the opposite corner is the **University Church** (Egyetemi templom), built in 1725–42 by monks of the Order of St Paul, with a rich, baroque interior. Along the quiet street called Szerb utca is the 18th-century **Serbian Orthodox Church** of St George. It has an iconostasis – the screen that divides the nave from the sanctuary in Eastern Orthodox churches – with a large number of icons on display.

Kossuth Lajos turns into Szabadsajtó út as it approaches the river. On the right-hand side, along Március tér, is the oldest building in Pest, the **Inner City Parish Church** (Belvárosi templom), now hemmed into an undignified position by the Elizabeth Bridge. The soot-covered, baroque exterior is unremarkable, but the handsome interior is far more interesting. It was founded in the 12th century, and some Romanesque elements are still visible. So, too, is the influence of the Turks, who turned the church into a

Pest's University buildings

mosque and carved a mihrab (prayer niche) on the chancel wall, facing Mecca. Next to the church is all that remains of the ancient Roman defences of Contra-Aquincum – an excavated square with a display of tablets and reliefs from the site.

The Little Boulevard

You won't find **Kiskörút** – the so-called Little Boulevard – named on a map, but it follows the line of the old city walls and encloses the district of Belváros. A medieval town grew around the Roman defence post on the site, evolving into a long, narrow strip that is boxed in by the Danube to the west and defensive walls on the other sides. The city walls were later replaced by three roads (**Károly körút**, **Múzeum körút** and **Vámház körút**), which are now known collectively as Kiskörút. The boulevard stretches right the way from Deák Ferenc tér to the Liberty Bridge. If you want to see the whole strip in comfort, it's best to take a tram (No. 47 or 49). There are several places of interest en route.

> **The vast Budapest Central Market Hall was designed and erected by the firm of Gustav Eiffel, who built the Eiffel Tower in Paris, so take note of the distinctive ironwork.**

The **Central Market Hall** (Vásárcsarnok; open Mon 6am–5pm, Tues–Fri 6am–6pm, Sat 6am–2pm) is on Vámház körút, by the Szabadság híd (Liberty Bridge), and was built here because the excellent transport links ensured the arrival of fresh produce. The hall was restored in 1996 and displays interesting historical photographs of the building. It now has a supermarket on the lower level, the ground floor sells vegetables, fruit, spices, meat and dairy produce, and there are handicrafts upstairs. There's a busy self-service cafe, the **Fakanál étterem**, selling heaped helpings of good, fresh Hungarian food at modest prices. It's a friendly, homely place with a fiddler providing suitable musical accompaniment. Nearby, there are several other food and wine stalls.

The boulevard continues through Kálvin tér, with the statue of Calvin dwarfed by coloured cafe umbrellas, to Múzeum körút, dominated by the **Hungarian National Museum** (Magyar Nemzeti Múzeum; open Tues–Sun 10am–6pm; admission charge). It was Hungary's first public collection and it remains the country's largest museum. Built in 1846 in neo-classical style with Corinthian columns and a sculpted tympanum, the museum stands back off the road in its own garden. Inside, amid monumental architectural and ornamental details, the whole story of Hungary unfolds – from the prehistoric history of the Carpathian Basin right up to the 21st century. On display are prehistoric remains, ancient jewellery and tools, Roman mosaics, a 17th-century Turkish tent fitted out with grand carpets, a baroque library, and some royal regalia, although the crown, orb, sceptre and sword have now been installed in the Houses of Parliament *(see page 59)*.

On Rákóczi út (just off Múzeum körút), is the celebrated **Uránia cinema** (Uránia Nemzeti Filmszínház; <www.urania-nf.hu>). Built in 1895, it was restored in 2002 and its façade, a mix of Venetian Gothic and Moorish styles, is looking radiant. It shows Hungarian and European art-house films and some international blockbusters, and is a centre for film festivals and cultural events.

Jewish Budapest

Back on the Little Boulevard, at the start of **Dohány utca** (Tobacco Street), you can't miss the enormous synagogue in flamboyant, Byzantine-Moorish style. The **Great Synagogue** (Nagy Zsinagóga; open Mon–Fri 10am–3pm, Sun 10am–1pm; admission charge) dates from the mid-19th

The monumental interior of the National Museum

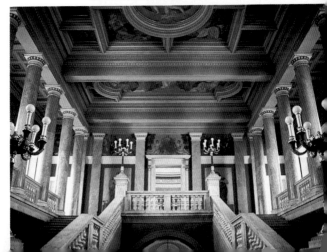

century, and is crowned by two onion-shaped copper domes. Before World War II, there were 125 synagogues in Budapest. This one is claimed to be the largest in Europe (the second largest in the world, after one in New York) and can accommodate up to 3,000 people. The great organ has been played by Liszt and Saint-Saens. The synagogue suffered severe war damage and was renovated between 1991 and 1996.

The adjoining **Jewish Museum** (Zsidó Múzeum; Dohány utca 2; Mon–Thurs 10am–5pm, Fri and Sun 10am–2pm) contains artefacts and treasures relating to the community,

The vast, spectacular dome of the Great Synagogue

mostly to Jewish festivals, together with an exhibit about the holocaust in Hungary. In a courtyard is the Raoul Wallenberg memorial garden, with a metal weeping willow tree, by the artist Imre Varga. Each leaf bears the name of one of the Budapest families who perished in the Holocaust. The site lies above the mass graves of Jews who were executed by the fascist Arrow Cross Government that was installed by the Nazis in 1944–5.

Despite the tragic events memorialised here, a visit to this community is inspiring. The area is thriving; there are about 80,000 Jewish residents, the children attend

Jewish schools, and Yiddish is studied at the University of Budapest.

The founder of Modern Zionism, Theodore Herzl (1860–1904), was born in a house on the site where the museum now stands.

The area surrounding the Great Synagogue (between Király utca and Wesselényi utca) was the heart of the old Jewish community, and the junction of Rumbach

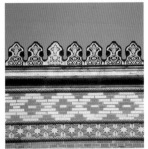

**The crenellated walls
of the Great Synagogue**

sebestyén utca and Dob utca was the entrance to the ghetto. There are still a number of interesting buildings and some patisseries and restaurants – the latter both kosher and non-kosher – that merit closer scrutiny here.

Leopold Town

Bounded by József Attila utca to the south and by Bajcsy-Zsilinszky út to the east, **Leopold Town** (Lipótváros) lies just north of the inner city. Directly opposite the approach to the Chain Bridge is Roosevelt tér, a square named after the former US president. Gresham Palace, the grand art nouveau building facing the square, was built in 1907 for an insurance company, and is now the Four Seasons Gresham Palace, a luxury hotel. Several similar buildings in Budapest have been converted into hotels: the Adria Palace is now Le Meridien, and the New York Insurance Company's building is being converted into the New York Palace. The statue in the centre of Roosevelt Square is of Ferenc Deák, who brokered the compromise establishing the Austro-Hungarian Empire during the 19th century *(see page 18)*.

Basilica of St Stephen

The **Basilica of St Stephen** (Szent István Bazilika; open daily 7am–7pm, except during services) is three blocks east of Roosevelt tér, and its 96-m (315-ft) dome dominates the skyline. Completed in 1905, after half a century of work, it is the largest church in Budapest; it can hold 8,500 people, and is often full to capacity. Before going inside, make the climb (or take the lift) to the top of the dome for Pest's highest viewpoint (exactly equal in height to the dome of the Houses of Parliament). In a reliquary in a rear chapel is the Szent Jobb (Holy Right), the much-revered, somewhat macabre mummified right hand of St Stephen.

Szabadság tér (Independence Square), a short walk to the north, is home to what is arguably Pest's finest architectural ensemble. At the centre is an obelisk dedicated to the Soviet troops who fell in the city, but the impressive buildings sur-

Looking heavenwards in St Stephen's Basilica

rounding the square are what really steal the show. The superb, lemon-coloured art nouveau building at No. 12 is now the American embassy. South of the embassy is the **Hungarian National Bank** and former **Postal Savings Bank** building, a lovely example of Secessionist (art nouveau) architecture. Built in 1901, it is decorated with glazed ceramic tiles and floral mosaics.

A spiral staircase leads up to the dome of St Stephen's

Across the square is the former Stock Exchange, now the national TV headquarters (it's called MTV but it has nothing to do with the airing of music videos), an eclectic-style building designed by the architect of the National Bank. In the film version of *Evita* it served as the Argentine presidential building, the Casa Rosada. All these buildings have interesting reliefs, a great contrast to the towers of polished granite of the new commercial complex that will be their neighbour on Szabadság tér. When completed, the complex will house offices, shops and food courts.

Houses of Parliament and Ethnographic Museum

The great dome of the **Houses of Parliament** (Országház), where the national government holds its sessions, is clearly visible from the square. The Parliament, designed by Imre Steindl, was built between 1885 and 1904 to symbolise the grandeur of the Austro-Hungarian Empire. When completed, it was the largest parliament building in the world: 268m (880ft) long, with 691 rooms, and 29 staircases. The architect may not have had London's Houses of Parliament in

mind, but the neo-Gothic arches and turrets rarely escape comparison with those of Westminster.

Located just opposite the Houses of Parliament is the city's **Ethnographic Museum** (Néprajzi Múzeum; open Tues–Sun 10am–6pm; admission charge). Built in 1893 to house the Supreme Court of Justice, it is worth a visit for the palatial interior alone. But it is also a great museum, and the exhibits of Hungarian folk art, crafts, rural life and dress are fascinating. A video, showing how people used to dress in wonderfully complex embroidered layers, is a revelation, and there are hands-

Imre Nagy immortalised, with the Houses of Parliament behind

on opportunities to learn traditional crafts, too. The temporary exhibitions are also usually excellent.

The eternal flame outside the Parliament Building was lit in 1996, the 40th anniversary of the 1956 Hungarian revolution. The statue of **Imre Nagy**, in an overcoat and hat, stands gazing into the flame. He was the prime minister executed for his part in the revolution.

Andrássy Út

Modelled on the Champs-Elysées in Paris, **Andrássy út** was driven straight through the city in the 1870s. Almost 2.5-km (1-mile) long, it connects the inner city to Városliget, the

City Park *(see page 68)*. There's an interesting walk from the castle to City Park (information booklet from Tourinform). The avenue is lined with some of Budapest's finest architecture, although many buildings are in need of repair and restoration. The elegance of the leafy avenue belies the prosaic nature of its former names – it has been known variously as Népköztársaság útja (People's Republic Avenue), Sugár út (Radial Road) and even, to the disgust of Budapestis, as Stalin út.

You can visit one of the large late 19th-century aristocratic homes at No. 3, at the beginning of the avenue, now home to the **Postal Museum** (Postamúzeum; open Tues–Sun 10am–6pm; admission charge). It has some colourful and interesting exhibits, such as correspondence between Thomas Edison

The Crown Jewels

The crown jewels (St Stephen's crown, orb, sceptre and sword) were installed in Parliament on 1 January 2000, the 1,000th anniversary of the coronation of King Stephen. They had been housed in the National Museum and the move was controversial as it was seen as an attempt to alter the crown's status from museum relic to living icon: an embodiment of the sovereignty of Hungary. The famous crown is romantically associated with St Stephen, but is actually of a slightly later date (the lower half is 11th century, the upper, 12th century). The treasures have had a history of being stolen, grabbed, pawned, seized, buried or lost, and of reappearing. After World War II, they ended up in Fort Knox and were restored to Hungary in 1978.

Visitors are admitted on guided tours to certain parts of the building, when Parliament is not in session. Tours begin to the right of the main stairs and enter through the grandiose central stairway to a splendid, 16-sided domed hall, then into the lobby, and finally into the principal debating chamber of the House.

**Bronze statue of the composer
Franz Liszt in flamboyant pose**

and the Hungarian tele-communications pioneer, Tivadar Puskás, but the real attraction is the building it-self, particularly the stair-way and balcony decorated with outstanding frescoes.

Located further up the avenue, at No. 22, is the neo-Renaissance **Hungar-ian State Opera House** (Magyar Állami Operaház; guided tours daily at 3pm and 4pm in several lan-guages, subject to perfor-mances). Completed in 1884 by Miklós Ybl, this is the most admired building on the avenue. Its Italianate style and restrained proportions fit exquisitely with its sur-roundings. The opulent gilt and marble interior is splendid and the architecture, atmos-phere and acoustics rank among the very best in Europe. If you are an opera lover, try to get a ticket for a performance here (<www.opera.hu>).

The artistic theme continues at **Dreschler House**, an art nouveau building just across the street and once home to the State Ballet. Down the small street to the right is the **New Theatre**, topped by a colourful piece of geometric art nou-veau embellishment.

No. 29 Andrássy út should not be overlooked. It is **Művész kávéház**, purveyors of fine confectionery since 1887, where you can get coffee in elegant surroundings.

The pedestrian-only block called **Liszt Ferenc tér** holds a number of theatres, restaurants and chic cafes. In the middle is an excellent modern statue of Liszt, portrayed in action, almost a caricature, with flailing hands and wild, windswept hair. The **Academy of Music**, completed in 1907, is at the end of the street. This art nouveau gem has a handsome façade, lobby and interior. It is quite easy to look inside when a concert isn't scheduled; alternatively, you could attend a performance here.

Cross the busy junction of Oktogon, and three streets north at Vörösmarty utca 35 you will find the **Franz Liszt Memorial Museum** (Liszt Ference Emlékmúzeum; open Mon–Fri 10am–6pm, Sat 9am–5pm; admission charge). This delightful little collection of pianos, memorabilia and period furnishings is kept in an apartment where the composer once lived. There are lots of lively bars and cafes around the museum, making it a good place for a break before continuing your tour of the area.

Franz Liszt

Franz (Ferenc) Liszt, composer and pianist, was born in 1811 in Raiding, Hungary, where his father, an amateur musician, was steward to the Esterházy family. As a boy Liszt studied in Vienna, then went to Paris, where he was lionised, and mixed with the most celebrated writers and artists of his day. He later worked in Weimar, Rome and Budapest, where he became president of the Academy of Music. Liszt was a complex man: torn between the adulation of audiences, the pleasures of fashionable society – including the company of beautiful women – and the desire for isolation in which to compose great works, he vacillated between the two worlds. In the latter part of his life he became religious and took minor orders in the church. He died in Bayreuth in 1886.

House on Andrássy út

Back on Andrássy út, at No. 60, is the **House of Terror** (Terror Háza; open Tues–Fri 10am–6pm, Sat–Sun 10am–7.30pm; admission charge). You can't miss it: the word 'terror' is cut out from an awning around the roof, and the sun shines through, projecting the word onto the side of the grey building. Allied to Hitler, the Hungarian Arrow Cross Party was responsible for exterminating Jews in World War II, some in this building, which later became the Nazi headquarters, then that of the communist secret police. It isn't a museum displaying artefacts, but a centre demonstrating the harshness of totalitarianism. It concludes by documenting the end of the Soviet era, the re-burial of Nagy, the Pope's visit and the fact that the perpetrators of so much suffering were never brought to justice. Stark and uncompromising, it leaves an indelible impression.

At No. 69 Andrássy út is the **Puppet Theatre** (Babszinház), one of the largest of its kind, which puts on some excellent performances for adults and children.

Stop for refreshment at the gracious **Lukács Cukrászda** at No. 70, one of the most attractive cafes in Budapest. It opened in 1912 and its crystal chandeliers and soft carpets preserve the ambience of that era. This is just the spot to sample some Hungarian delicacies – *Eszterházy torta*, perhaps – while listening to live music in the afternoon.

As Andrássy út edges closer to the City Park, the villas and mansions in garden settings get noticeably grander. Many of them now house embassies. **Kodály körönd** (a square named after Hungarian composer, Zoltán Kodály) is a splendid ensemble, its curving façades decorated with classical figures and inlaid motifs. At No. 1 there is an archive and museum devoted to the composer (open Wed 10am–4pm, Thur–Sat 10am–6pm, Sun 10am–2pm; admission charge).

At Andrássy út 103 is the **Ferenc Hopp Museum of Far Eastern Art** (Hopp Ferenc Kelet-ázsiai Múzeum; open Tues–Sun 10am–6pm; admission charge). Hopp was a businessman who, by the time of his death in 1919, had amassed a vast collection of pieces. Some 20,000 exotic items are on display. The **György Ráth Museum** (Ráth György Múzeum; Városligeti fasor 12; open Tues–Sun 10am–6pm; admission charge), which displays more of Hopp's treasures as well as items from the Museum of Applied Arts, lies south of here, in a handsome art nouveau villa.

The unmistakeable façade of the House of Terror

A hero in Heroes' Square

Heroes' Square

Andrássy út ends in a burst of pomp at **Heroes' Square** (Hősök tere), a huge, open space housing the **Millennium Monument**, built on the 1,000th anniversary of the Magyar settlement of the region. The 36-m (118-ft) column supports the figure of the Archangel Gabriel who, according to legend, appeared to St Stephen in a dream and offered him the crown of Hungary. Around the pedestal sit Prince Arpád and the Magyar tribal chiefs on horseback, while flanking the column is a semi-circular colonnade with statues of historical figures, starting with King Stephen. In front of the statuary is the Tomb of the Unknown Soldier. The communist-era demonstrations that took place here have given way to youthful skateboarders who hang out at the base of the monument and bob and weave through cones around the square.

Facing each other across Heroes' Square are two large neoclassical structures that are near mirror images of each

> other. On the right is the **Műcsarnok** (Palace of Art; open Tues–Wed 10am–6pm, Thur noon–8pm, Fri–Sun 10am–6pm; admission charge), which mounts high-quality temporary exhibitions of work by contemporary Hungarian and foreign artists and also has a fine bookstore. Outside, a splendid pediment crowns the building with a mosaic of St Stephen in his role as patron saint of the arts. There is also a smaller sister branch of the museum in the City Park.

Located just behind Műcsarnok is the **world's biggest hourglass**, which was unveiled at midnight on 30 April–1 May 2004 to mark Hungary's entry to the European Union. It's a huge wheel, 8m (26ft) in diameter, and weighing 40-tonnes. Made of Indian granite carved in Italy and Swiss steel, the clock turns once a year, in a half circle, setting the sand running anew, to usher in the new year.

Opposite Műcsarnok is the **Museum of Fine Arts** (Szépművészeti Múzeum; open Tues–Sun 10am–5.30pm; admission charge) holding the city's most highly regarded and wide-ranging collection. It begins chronologically with Greek, Roman and Egyptian treasures but the most significant section is that of European art from 1300–1800. There are some 2,500 masterpieces, of which some 800 are on show at any one time. Italian, Dutch, German and Spanish schools are all superbly

Hungarian Playing Cards

Not hearts, diamonds, clubs and spades but leaves, bells, acorns and hearts: Hungary has its own style of playing cards, designed in Budapest in 1830 by József Schneider, a prominent manufacturer of cards. The most popular are 'Tell cards' which feature characters from the tales about the legendary Swiss patriot, William Tell. There are other designs: royal personages of the Austro-Hungarian monarchy and medieval heroes are also popular.

Exhibit at the Museum of Fine Arts

represented. The latter is particularly notable, constituting one of the best collections of Spanish Old Masters outside Spain, with masterpieces by El Greco, Goya and others. There are also rooms dedicated to British, French, and Flemish artists. The 19th- to 20th-century collection includes a treasure trove of French Impressionist and Post-Impressionist artists such as Cézanne, Pisarro, Monet, Gauguin and Renoir. Leonardo da Vinci is featured in the prints and drawings sections, and the museum also possesses a bronze horseman by Leonardo.

City Park

Beyond Heroes' Square is the **City Park** (Városliget), a lovely green space where Budapestis stroll, picnic, hire boats and family-sized pedal-cars, go to the zoo and visit museums. The park, which covers some 100 hectares (250 acres), began to evolve in the early 19th century, although many of the present amenities were added during preparations for the Magyar Millennium festivities of 1896. Sir Winston Churchill and George Washington are represented among the statues.

Across the bridge over the boating lake, which doubles as an ice-skating rink in winter, lies the **Vajdahunyad Castle** (Vajdahunyad vára) It was a temporary building for the Millennium Exhibition in 1896 but proved so popular that it was rebuilt in permanent form. It reproduces part of the exterior of the fairy-tale Hunyadi Castle in Transylvania, hence the name, but it is also a catalogue of Hungarian architectural history – Gothic, Romanesque, baroque, it's all here. Inside the castle is the **Hungarian Agricultural Museum** (Mezőgazdasági Múzeum; open Tues–Sun 9am–5pm; admission charge) housing a comprehensive collection illustrating the history of Hungarian horse-breeding, hunting, fishing, and farming. If you want to see the castle at its best, return at night, when it is beautifully illuminated.

Within the grounds, there is a **Catholic church** (Ják Chapel) with a Romanesque portal (another reconstruction) and one of the city's favourite statues. Called *Anonymous*, it depicts the medieval chronicler who gave Hungary its first written records. The scribe's face is hidden inside the cowl of his habit; aspiring writers seek inspiration by touching his pen.

Also within the park are the zoo, a spa complex and two amusement parks. In the northeast corner of the park is the **Vidám Amusement Park** (Budapesti Vidámpark), an old-fashioned, funfair-style amusement park for children. You won't find huge, scary rides here, just low-tech carousels, dodgems and a Ferris wheel. One carousel dates from 1906 and the wooden roller coaster was opened in 1922. Adjoining it is a mini-version of the park, suitable for younger children. Next door to the amusement parks, a circus makes regular appearances throughout the year.

In the northwest corner of the park, the **Zoo** (Állatkert), one of the oldest in the world (1866), welcomes visitors with an art nouveau entrance decorated with polar bears and elephants. The recently restored Elephant House is a handsome Oriental-Hungarian construction with a tall minaret. Renovations on several pavilions have produced more grounds where animals can roam freely. The Palm House, the largest tropical hall in Central Europe, reopened at the end of 2000.

Next to the zoo is Gundel, a fine restaurant that is legendary in Hungarian culinary circles.

Also in the northwest corner is the jewel in the park, the **Széchenyi Baths** complex (Széchenyi fürdő; open May–Sept daily 6am–7pm; Oct–Apr till 5pm). One of the largest medicinal bath complexes in Europe, it provides year-round, open-air swimming, at a constant temperature of 27°C (81°F), in beautiful surroundings. The neo-baroque buildings, bright yellow and topped by a series of green domes, opened in 1881. Inside the pool area, surrounded by ivy-clad walls and sumptuous statuary, groups of men stand up to their chests in warm water amid the steam, concentrating

intently on games of chess (the chess boards form part of the small jetties that protrude into the pool).

The **Transport Museum** (Közlekedési Múzeum; open Tues–Fri 10am–5pm, Sat–Sun 10am–6pm; admission charge), which borders the eastern side of the park, at the corner of Hermina út and Ajtósi Dürer sor, is signalled by the trains that appear to be roaring right out of the building, not to mention the plane on the roof. Inside you will find all kinds of transport, from horse-drawn carriages to Soviet space-age equipment.

Anybody keen on architecture should keep their eyes peeled near City Park for splendid examples of art nouveau. One unusually shaped building is home to the **National Association for the Blind** (Hermina út 47).

Another, slightly more out of the way, is the **Geology Institute** (Stefánia út 14), a marvellous structure topped by blue tiles and statues of Atlas supporting globes. Try to see the lobby if it is open. Another terrific example of the style is the **Egger Villa** (Városligeti fasor 24).

The Great Boulevard

The bustling **Great Boulevard** (Nagykörút) forms a long, sweeping arc from Margaret Bridge to the Petőfi Bridge. It doesn't appear on the map because it has five different names along its 3-km (2-mile) length: Szent István körút, Teréz körút, Erzsébet körút, Jószef körút and Ferenc körút. The city planners

Chess at Széchenyi baths

approved the project and pushed it through for the Magyar Millennium year of 1896.

The boat moored close to the Petőfi bridge, the **A38**, is a hip club and restaurant. It opened in April 2003 and is a venue for music, cultural and other events, many of them international: anything from the Asian Dub Foundation to Klezmer music. The name A38 refers to its former life as a Ukranian stone carrier, **Artemorszk 38**. It is open day and night and, apart from elegance and sophistication, good food and music, it also offers a warm welcome and even provides toys and high-chairs for children.

➤   The architectural pride of the Great Boulevard is the **Museum of Applied and Decorative Arts** (Iparművészeti Múzeum; open Tues–Sun 10am–6pm; admission charge), just off Ferenc körút at Nos 33–37 Üllői út. The splendid art nouveau exterior incorporates Hungarian folk art and majolica tiles. Huge green Oriental cupolas, small spiky towers, a majolica lantern and a bright green-and-gold tiled roof crown the edifice. The museum's architect, Ödön Lechner (who also built the Postal Savings Bank in Leopold Town), is seen as the greatest exponent of this Magyar style.

> The Hungarian holocaust was the largest and fastest deportation of all: in just 56 days, some 437,402 Jewish citizens were deported, all but 15,000 to Dr Mengele at Auschwitz. A third of the victims of Auschwitz were Hungarian citizens. In all, somewhere between 450,000 and 600,000 Hungarians perished.

The interior is just as remarkable: Hungarian with strong Moorish influences. Shimmering white arches, balconies and swirling staircases sweep up to a fine art nouveau skylight. The main hall is covered by a great expanse of glass supported by an iron frame, and ferns and potted plants around the hall create a kind of winter garden. A fascinating permanent exhibition, showing the progress of arts and crafts techniques from the 12th century, is augmented by temporary exhibitions on more specialised subjects. There are striking examples of work in a variety of media – textiles, ceramics, metal-work, leather and wood. The section on art nouveau from across the world is particularly attractive.

Holocaust Memorial Centre

Across Ferenc körút, further up Üllői utca is Páva utca, the location of the **Holocaust Memorial Centre** (Holokauszt Emlékközpont; open Tues–Sun 10am–6pm). Secu-

Engraved glass by Julia Bathony, Museum of Decorative Arts

rity is tight at the centre, which opened on 16 April 2004, the 60th anniversary of the Hungarian holocaust. At the opening, the director was uncompromising: 'This is not a Jewish institution. It is a Hungarian institution, founded and funded by the Hungarian Government.' The synagogue originally on the site has been restored, and new wings, designed by István Mányi, have been added. The centre has permanent exhibitions as well as being a memorial and an education and research centre. There is a wall on which the names of the victims are recorded. At the centre's opening, the Prime Minister at the time, Péter Medgyessy, described the holocaust as 'a hideous crime committed by the Hungarian people against Hungarian people'.

The Café New York

An Historic Cafe and a Panoramic View

Just beyond Erzsébet körút, at Hársfa utca 47, the **Philatelic Museum** (Bélyeg Múzeum; open Tues–Sun 10am–6pm, Oct–Mar 10am–4pm; admission charge) contains every stamp issued by Hungary since 1871. It also displays some interesting misprints, including an upside-down Madonna and child.

Teréz körút and Erzsébet körút have traditionally been centres of Budapest's cultural, as well as its commercial, life. At the junction of Erzséber körút and Dohány utca is the **Café New York** (formerly known as the Hungaria), the neo-baroque and art nouveau interior of which is currently being restored. The cafe's artistic heyday was at the turn of the 19th century, followed by a revival in the 1930s; however, it suffered wartime damage and was rammed by a tank in 1956. During the socialist period, the place was reputed to have had the slowest, most disagreeable staff in Budapest. It is due to re-open in 2006.

Further along, where Teréz körút intersects with Váci utca, is Nyugati railway station – another triumph for Gustav Eiffel. The modern building next door is the Westend Shopping Centre, and the **Budapest Panorama Balloon** is tethered to its roof. It ascends to a height to 150m (500ft) and offers fine views over the city; trips last about 15–20 minutes (summer 10am–midnight; rest of year 10am–6pm).

MARGARET ISLAND

Walk onto **Margaret Island** (Margitsziget) from the tram stop on Margaret Bridge, and you'll be greeted by a fountain and the centenary monument by István Kiss, unveiled in 1972 for the centenary of the union of Buda and Pest. Visitors enjoy the thermal facilities and treatments offered at two hotels on the island; Budapestis come to walk, bike, play tennis and eat picnics, and, on sunny afternoons, enjoy the enormous outdoor **Palatinus Baths** complex, with thermal pools and a wave pool. A beautiful rose garden blooms in front of the baths and nearby is an open-air stage *(see below)*.

Margaret Island is 2km (1¼ miles) long and only a few hundred metres/yards at the widest point. Many of its 10,000 trees are now more than a century old, and large areas of the island have been landscaped. To preserve the island's peace and quiet, cars are prohibited, which comes as a pleasant relief if you are looking for a tranquil break from the city.

Alongside a landmark octagonal water tower is an open-air theatre, where concerts, opera and ballet performances are presented in the summer. Nearby are the ruins of a 13th-century **Dominican Convent** founded by King Béla IV. The king enrolled his 11-year-old daughter, Margit, at the convent in fulfilment of a vow he had made, should he survive the Mongol invasion. Princess (later St) Margit remained on the island for the rest of her life, and a marble plaque marks her burial place.

CITY OUTSKIRTS

Statue and Rail Heritage Parks

The **Statue Park** (Szoborpark Múzeum; <www.szoborpark.hu>; open daily 10am–dusk; admission charge) is a slightly surreal park where some of the monumental statues once imposed by the communist regime on the streets of Budapest are displayed. Rather than see them destroyed, the authorities decided to put them here, in a suburban setting. Giant socialist-realist figures of Lenin and anonymous worker heroes strut against the backdrop of newly-built homes.

To get to the park, start from Deák tér *(see page 50)*, where you take tram No. 49 to the Etele tér terminus then buy a ticket from the Volánsbusz building and get the yellow Volánbusz from Stall 7–8, going to Diósd Érd. After about 15 minutes you will see, on your right, a red-brick portico framing massive statues of Lenin, Marx and Stalin.

Lenin stands tall, Statue Park

Train aficionados should love Budapest's **Rail Heritage Park** (Magyar Vasúttörténeti Park; open Tues–Sun Apr–Oct 10am–6pm, Nov–mid-Dec 10am–3pm; admission charge), designed as an inter-active space dedicated to trains and railways. To get there, you have to make the 15-minute journey on the shuttle train called the *különvonat* from Nyugati railway station. This service runs from early April to late October, during the hours the park is open. The park has about 70 vintage steam locomotives and coaches for children of all ages to play on, including rare, rotating loading docks.

EXCURSIONS

A short distance north of Budapest, the Danube dramatically alters its easterly course for a southern tack. The prosaic name of this extraordinary region is Dunakanyar, meaning the Danube Bend. Here the river is at its most alluring, the countryside lush and unspoiled, and there are delightful historic towns to explore. **Szentendre**, **Visegrád** and **Ezstergom** can be visited in one trip. If you fancy going further afield, you could take a trip to the **Lake Balaton** area – Hungary's seaside; to the Puszta, the Great Plain; or even up the Danube to Vienna (it takes five hours and hydrofoils go daily).

Szentendre

Szentendre is a honey-pot with numerous souvenir and art and craft shops and stalls. It's known for its churches, artists' colony and many small museums and galleries (close to 100 in total). Tourinform at Dumtsa J. utca 22 will provide you with details. The easiest way to reach the town (about 20km (12m from the city) is by HÉV suburban railway from Batthyány tér in Buda. In summer, boats make a five-hour journey all the way from Budapest to Esztergom, stopping en route at Szentendre and Visegrád. An alternative, giving a wonderful bird's-eye view, is a 25-minute helicopter trip over the area.

Serbian refugees twice settled in Szentendre in the wake of Turkish invasions: first in the late 13th century, and again in 1690. On the latter occasion, around 8,000 Serbs brought their religion, art, architecture and commercial acumen with them. These days, the area between Budapest and Szentendre is mainly commuting country.

The majestic Serbian church on the hill is the town's most prominent landmark. The town centre, **Fő tér**, is a picture-postcard square that remains pretty much as it was in the 18th century, lined with houses that once belonged to wealthy burghers. The Serbian community erected the iron, rococo memorial cross in the centre of the plaza in 1763, in gratitude for being spared by the plague.

The rust-red, 18th-century **Serbian Orthodox Church** perched on the hill is only open for services, but within its grounds is the excellent **Collection of Serbian Ecclesiastical Art**, displaying precious carvings, icons and manuscripts. The oldest church in the town lies just above here on top of the hill, affording a perfect vantage point from which to peer down into the tiny gardens and courtyards and across the rooftops.

Skansen

A unusual attraction can be found 4km (2 miles) from Szentendre – **Skansen**, the **Hungarian Open Air Village Museum** (Szabadtéri Néprajzi Múzeum; open Apr–Oct 9am–5pm; admission charge). Skansen, the name of the original Swedish

---

Turul Birds

Turul birds are mythical eagles and they are a powerful Hungarian symbol, sometimes shown carrying the flaming sword of God. The bird is said to have sired both Attila the Hun and Álmos, father of Árpád, who led the Magyar conquest of the Carpathian Basin in the 9th century. The link with Attila gave Árpád the right to reconquer his lands. The best-known example of a turul is probably the one at Szent György tér, next to the upper terminal of the Budavári Sikló (funicular.) You can spot four more on top of the Liberty Bridge.

village museum, has been naturalised into Hungarian. Catch the No. 8 bus departing from the terminal next to the HÉV station, or take one of the buses from the Tourinform office, on the road from the bus station to the centre of Szentendre. The 46-hectare (115-acre) museum site contains villages of genuine houses, churches, mills, farm buildings, workshops and smithies, dating mostly from the late-18th to the early 20th century, and gathered from across Hungary. Live demonstrations by craftspeople bring to life village traditions.

A cheerful country woman

Visegrád

Upstream, where the Danube truly bends, lies **Visegrád** (meaning 'High Castle'), which is accessible by boat or bus from Szentendre. The finest place to enjoy the views – reminiscent of the Rhine – is the citadel, high on a hill above the ruins of the old palace of Visegrád.

The strategic value of a site commanding the river bend was appreciated as early as the 4th century, when the Romans built a fort here. In the 14th century, the Angevin kings of Hungary built a **palace** on the site, each monarch adding new rooms and piling on opulence until the building covered an area now estimated at some 18 hectares (45 acres). When King Mátyás *(see page 15)* lived here, the palace was famous throughout Europe as an 'earthly paradise'. Between 1462 and 1475, Vlad the Impaler (on whom the Dracula legend was partly based) was held prisoner here.

Like the Royal Palace in Buda, the palace of Visegrád fell into ruin during the Turkish occupation (although it was not captured and destroyed by the Turks) and was eventually forgotten. Excavations began in 1930; part of the main building has been unearthed and certain parts have been rebuilt (using materials that are obviously new, to differentiate these sections from the original ones). Among the best of the discoveries are the superb Hercules Fountain (a rare vestige of Hungarian Renaissance architecture), the vaulted galleries of the Court of Honour, and the restored Lion's Fountain. The hexagonal tower on the hillside is known as the Tower of Solomon. Topping it all is the **citadel**, once considered so impregnable that the Hungarian crown jewels were kept here.

> A small museum inside Visegrád's citadel may appeal to those with a love of the macabre – it has life-size models of medieval executions, including beheading and burning-at-the-stake.

Esztergom

Esztergom, a further 20km (12 miles) upriver, lacks the picturesque charm (and the tourists) of Szentendre, but is historically important. It is linked by hydrofoil to Budapest, and by boat or bus to Szentendre and Visegrád. Take the boat if you have a couple hours to spare, as the river's most scenic stretch lies between Visegrád and Esztergom.

King Stephen was born in Esztergom, which was then the capital of Hungary. The town remains the religious centre of the country and has the largest church in the land. The massive **basilica** stands on the site of an 11th-century church where Stephen was crowned in 1000. That church was destroyed in battle against the Turks. The only atmospheric part of the current building is the rather spooky crypt.

The most valuable part of the basilica is the red-marble side chapel called the **Bakócz-kápolna** – a pure example of Italian Renaissance. Built in the 16th century, the chapel, salvaged from the ruins around it and reassembled in the 19th century, is all that survives of the original basilica. A highlight of the basilica is the **treasury** (closed Nov–Apr, as is the tower), which contains Hungary's richest collection of religious objects. A climb up the tower takes you from priceless treasures to priceless views. Esztergom unfolds beneath your feet, and on clear days you can also see all the way to Slovakia.

Alongside the basilica, the remains of a medieval royal palace have been excavated and restored to form the **Castle Museum**. Among the highlights are St Stephen's Hall, the frescoed Hall of Virtues, and the 12th-century Royal Chapel.

The most interesting collection in Esztergom lies at the foot of Basilica Hill, on the riverside. The **Christian Museum** (Keresztény Múzeum; open Tues–Sun Mar 10am–5pm, Apr–Oct 10am–6pm) is one of the best museums of religious art in the country. Covering the Gothic and Renaissance periods from the 13th–16th centuries, it has a number of

Esztergom's basilica

excellent 14th- and 15th-century Italian paintings. Also notable is the 15th-century coffin of Garamszentbenedek, an intricately carved and painted devotional vehicle, once paraded through the streets at Easter.

Lake Balaton

Hungary has no coastline so **Lake Balaton** is the next best thing. This massive freshwater lake – at 77km (48 miles) across, with an area of nearly 600 sq. km (230 sq. miles) it is the largest lake in central and western Europe – is surrounded by verdant hills, orchards, vineyards, and historic villages. The northwestern tip of Balaton lies about 100km (62 miles) from Budapest. In winter the lake freezes over completely, while in summer the shallow water warms quickly, but is subject to wind-driven waves; when a storm blows up even the ferries call it a day. The mildly alkaline

Tihany, on Lake Balaton

water (considered good for the health) attracts swimmers by the thousands. Many holidaymakers avail themselves of the services of local medicinal baths, spa and wellness hotels.

On the north shore, **Balatonfüred** has been a spa since Roman times, and has an internationally regarded cardiac hospital. In season, this is one of the lake's liveliest resorts.

Other attractive parts of the lake include the **Tihany peninsula**, which has National Park status, and the Badacsony region – an important wine-producing area. The latter is fascinating because of its volcanic past, which is evident as soon as you catch sight of the conical green hills. Mt Badacsony, the central basalt peak and, at 437m (1,434ft), the largest of the extinct volcanoes, is invariably described as 'coffin-shaped'.

Keszthely (pronounced 'kest-hey') is the site of the Festetics family's palace (open all year round); one of Hungary's most important baroque monuments . The highlight is the Helikon library, claimed to be the grandest in the country, and it alone is worth the palace entrance charge.

Continuing out of Keszthely to the southwest on Highway 71, you reach another good historical collection. The **Balaton Museum** portrays the story of the settlement of the lake and the development of its people, including their agricultural and fishing practices, and the lake's flora and fauna.

Near the southwest corner of the lake, **Kis-Balaton** (Little Balaton), a marshy National Reserve, is noted for its rare birdlife. Observation towers are provided for birdwatchers.

The south shore is popular among holidaymakers, and there are several resorts. The largest town on the south coast is **Siófok**, which has attractive beach and lively nightlife. Pleasure craft depart from the large harbour, but the most appealing stretch of waterfront is to be found in the gardens immediately east of the port. The town centre is further east, just before the hotel zone.

WHAT TO DO

SPAS AND BATHS

You don't have to be suffering from a particular ailment to benefit from spa treatment, and there's nothing wrong with a little pampering when you are on holiday. In Hungary, so-called health and wellness hotels and centres are major attractions. The centres provide saunas and steam baths, therapy and relaxation, new-age treatments and alternative therapies, sport and exercise, gastronomy and a staggering number of beauty and style treatments. Some of them also offer dentistry and cosmetic surgery. Even shopping malls have wellness and beauty centres: you can emerge detoxified, mentally alert and looking good.

There are about 1,300 thermal springs in Hungary, and some 300 of them are used for bathing – around 130 are in Budapest. There's so much thermal water they use it to heat the houses, but it doesn't do much for the plumbing. Steam baths can be traced back to Roman times and the Ottomans established Turkish baths, some of which are still operational today. Massage was important and numerous different types of massage are available today.

While the spas all offer mineral waters, there is also medicinal water, which is known to have proven medical effects. Such water may ease joint pain, pain resulting from injuries, neuralgia, gout and rheumatism, but it may also be efficacious in helping people with skin conditions and gynaecological disorders. There are waters for bathing in and waters for drinking, which can be useful for alleviating digestive disorders and metabolic conditions. The relaxing treatments certainly relieve stress.

Swimming in opulent surroundings at the Gellért Hotel Baths

The health centres are carefully regulated. In autumn 2003, the Ministry of Economy and Transport published a decree on wellness hotels, laying down requirements to be observed, and the National Tourist Office *(see page 128 for addresses)* can provide information on approved centres and treatments. Doctors and trained assistants oversee treatments, as some techniques are contraindicated for patients with certain ailments, and medical approval is necessary to ensure that the bathing will be beneficial.

In Budapest, you have a choice: there are fitness and wellness hotels, or you can just visit the traditional baths and avail yourself of their services.

Of the traditional baths, the Gellért and the Széchenyi *(see pages 40 and 70)* are the grandest of them all, art nouveau and neoclassical palaces respectively, with splendid baths and outdoor pools. You can swim or have a mud treatment, massage or an underwater traction bath. The Gellért spa has recently been renovated and there are extensive medical services at the medicinal bath, although they specialise in rheumatology and pulmonology. There are spa services and an inhalatorium.

The Széchenyi Spa, one of Europe's largest bathing complexes, is to be found in Városliget (City Park). It also offers physiotherapy and has a rheumatology department. The adventure pool is fitted with a water chute, underwater aeration, neck massage and water-jet massage points. At the 16th-century Király and Rudas baths – Rac baths are closed at present – true local atmosphere can be appreciated. The ex-

> Aside from spa waters, there are also cave cures, in which clean air and high humidity aid respiratory conditions; and there are dry baths using carbon dioxide of volcanic origin to improve heart and circulatory conditions and skin complaints.

Baths are a place for socialising as well as health treatments

perience can be illuminating in these historic bath houses, where sunlight filters through holes in the domed ceilings, and stone arches ring the octagonal pools. By contrast, the Palatinus Strand on Margaret Island is more like a giant water park, and ideal for families.

SPORTS

Bowling: There are several bowling alleys, including one at the Duna Plaza shopping centre and two at the Novotel and Stadion hotels.

Cycling: Budapest has nearly 100km (62 miles) of bicycle paths throughout the city. You can pick up a copy of the *Budapest for Bikers* map at tourist offices *(see page 128)*. Bikes can be hired in City Park and on Margaret Island.

Equestrian sports: The members of the Hungarian Equestrian Tourism Association (<www.equi.hu>) provide riding, trekking, carriage driving and other activities.

Golf: Golfing greens are becoming very popular in Hungary. The Hungarian Golf Federation (<www.hungolf.hu>) provides all the necessary information. There are also driving ranges around the capital.

Golfers looking for convenience could try the Golf Country Service (Váci utca 19–21, tel: 318 8030, <www.golf service.hu>; open 9am–6pm). They arrange to collect you, take you to any of the courses near the capital, and then bring you back to Budapest.

Further afield, there is an 18-hole course at the northern end of the long, narrow Szentendre Island opposite Visegrád, about 35 km (22 miles) from Budapest.

Tennis: More than 100 tennis courts are located at hotels, hostels and camp sites. They charge 500–1,000HUF an hour. Information from the Hungarian Tennis Association, tel: 252-6687. Badminton and squash are also played. There are also courts at the Mammut shopping centre.

Watersports: Windsurfing and yachting are possible on Lake Balaton, and boards and boats can be hired at the main resorts. Motor boats, however, are prohibited.

Spectator Sports

The largest stadium is the Puskás Ferenc Stadion. Close by is the new Budapest Sportarena. The old stadium burned down and this new one is a modern structure that hosts pop concerts, etc, as well as sporting events. The nearest Metro is Stadionok (previously Népstadion).

Football: This is Hungary's biggest spectator sport. Two of the most popular of Budapest's first-division football teams are Kispest-Honvéd (who play at Bozsik stadium; tel: 282-9789) and Ferencváros (FTC stadium; tel: 215-1013).

Grand Prix: A major event is the annual Formula I Grand Prix meeting at the Hungaroring, around 19km (12 miles) east of Budapest.

SHOPPING

Budapest is no longer the bargain basement it once was, and although Hungarian pay packets are slim, prices for many goods are about the same as those in other European capitals. Shopping has undergone a revolution in Budapest in recent years, a major development being the proliferation of shopping malls – there are now more than 20 of them. The largest are the **Pólus Centre** (reached by bus from Keleti pu) and the **Westend City Centre** (Váci út 1–3; tel: 238-7777), next to Nyugati railway station. **Mammut** and **Mammut II** at Moszkva tér are great favourites with local residents. On the other side of town, **Árkád** is a pleasant, newish shopping centre located opposite the Örs Vezér tere metro terminal.

Hand-painted Easter eggs

The shopping centres are home to branches of many of the same chain stores that you find in other countries in Europe: C&A, Marks & Spencer, Debenhams, Benetton, Virgin Megastore, Esprit, Mango, Mexx, etc, as well as some local establishments.

The other major change in shopping patterns has been the arrival in great force of super- and hypermarkets. Tesco has become the leading supermarket in Hungary, with 26 hypermarkets and 27 supermarkets. Auchan, the French hypermarket, is also a visible presence.

What to Buy

Visitors' shopping expeditions often start on **Váci utca**, a pedestrianised boulevard with a wide selection of shops. For folk art and other handicrafts, try **Folkart Centrum** (Váci utca 58; tel: 318-5840). This branch, the biggest and best of a small chain of cooperative outlets, is open daily. The **Central Market Hall** (Vásárcsarnok) has an Aladdin's cave of colourful treasures, and there are plenty more outside on Fövám tér.

Ceramics and Porcelain: Hungary is celebrated for its ceramics and porcelain. The **Herend** factory has been producing fine porcelain since 1826 and has a shop at József Nádor tér 11 (behind the Gerbeaud Café on Vörösmarty tér; tel: 317-2622). **Zsolnay** porcelain is also world-famous. The shop is located at V. Kígyó utca 4 (tel: 318-3712), an area also good for antiques.

Traditional-style plates and vases come in distinctive blue and white; there are ochre and floral-decorated glazed water jars from Mezötúr, and local charcoal-coloured items, called 'black pottery'. Domestic pottery can be had at Herend Village Pottery (Bem rakpart 37).

Chess sets: You will find beautiful sets with pawns in the guise of foot soldiers, and knights as hussars in bright 18th-century garb.

Hungarian Embroidery

The oldest example of Hungarian embroidery is Stephen I's gold silk robe, now in the National Museum. Embroidery became a profession in medieval times and by the 16th century a style called *úrihímzés* was practised, the designs emanating from Renaissance Italy and Turkey. Hand-embroidered items can be bought at Folkart shops and at stalls. Look for intricate Halas lace, Matyó costumes, red-and-blue Palóc work (on aprons, towels and kerchiefs), and Kalocsa folk costumes. Prices can be high, as a great deal of handiwork is involved.

Woodwork: You will find a variety of children's toys, including puzzles and mobiles, made from wood, just like in the good old days. Boxes, bowls, walking sticks and other such items are also available.

Food and drink: Popular gifts include paprika in gift boxes or sachets; dried mushrooms, such as ceps and chanterelles; strudels packed in sturdy cardboard boxes; salami and goose-liver paté;

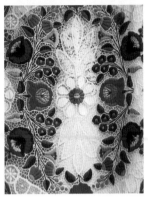

Intricate Hungarian lace-work

Hungarian wines (particularly Tokaj) and liqueurs, such as apricot brandy. The House of Hungarian Wines (Szentháromság tér 6; tel: 212-1031; open noon–8pm) stocks 700 different wines from 22 regions across the country and conducts tastings. The Budapest Wine Society (Battyány utca 59; tel: 212-2569) is another source.

ENTERTAINMENT

Tickets for theatre, opera, ballet, and classical concerts are more reasonably priced in Budapest than in many other cities, perhaps because Hungarians don't see the arts as highbrow and élitist.

Opera, Classical Music and Ballet

The **Hungarian State Opera House** on Andrássy út 20 is the finest of the city's dedicated opera venues and connoisseurs rank it among Europe's best. Tickets are available at the box office (tel: 332-7914; <www.opera.hu>). You can also purchase tickets online at <www.jegymester.hu>). Just around the corner from the Opera, the Budapesti Operett-színház (Nagymező utca 19; tel: 312-4866; <www.operett szinhaz.hu>) stages internationally known musicals as well as those written and produced in Hungary.

The city has a number of other fine halls *(színház)* for symphonies, concerts and opera, including the **Ferenc Liszt Academy of Music** (Liszt Ferenc tér 8; tel: 342-0179), a splendid art nouveau music hall built in 1904; and **Pesti Vigadó** (Vigadó tér 1; tel: 266-6177). The **Bartók Béla Memorial House** (Bartók Béla Emlékház; Csalán út 29; tel: 394-2100; <www.bartokmuseum.hu>), where the Bartók String Quartet sometimes give concerts, is an excellent place to enjoy music. **St Stephen's Basilica**, the **Houses of Parliament**, the **Hilton Hotel** and the **Castle** are also used as concert venues. In summer, concerts are held in various parks and gardens, and there are also performances on boats

The Hungarian State Opera House, one of the best in Europe

and concerts in cafes. Budapest has music for all tastes. The **Budapest Congress Centre** (Budapesti Kongressusi Központ; tel: 372-5400; <www.bcc.hu>) has a modern auditorium and doubles as a conference centre and music venue (check the website for programmes).

Opera and ballet are also performed at the **Erkel Theatre** (Köztársaság tér 30; tel: 333-0540).

Theatre

The **Nemzeti Színház** (National Theatre, Bajor Gizi Park 1; tel: 476-6800.) on Hevesi Sándor tér offers performances of Shakespeare and Ibsen in Hungarian. Apart from the English-language **Merlin Theatre** (Gerlóczy utca 4; tel: 266-4632), all plays are staged in Hungarian. The **Thália Theatre** (Nagymező utca 22–24; tel: 311-1874), recently overhauled and air-conditioned, offers a varied programme – from the *Vagina Monologues* to *West Side Story*.

Pop, Rock and Jazz

For pop, rock, and jazz concerts, see the weekly *Style* supplement of the *Budapest Sun* or the monthly publication *Where Budapest?*, or visit <www.pestiside.hu>. Both contain good round-ups of bars, pubs and clubs in the city. Ticket agencies are usually open Mon–Fri 10am–6pm and Sat mornings. **Ticket Express** (<www.tex.hu>) can be found at many locations in the city, including Andrássy út, Mammut and Ferenciek tere. **Publika** (Károly krt 9; tel: 322-2010), can help with concert and theatre tickets. Tickets for rock concerts and jazz clubs are available from **Music Mix**, Ferenciek tere 10.

Traditional Music and Dance

There's *klezmer*, which is based on traditional Jewish music improvised by informal groups of musicians, and there's *táncház*, an urban revival of traditional rural Magyar dance. Called a 'dance-house movement', it arose as an expression of protest and national pride during communist rule in the 1970s and has produced some of the biggest names in Hungarian folk music. The centre for contemporary, world, gypsy, jazz and folk music is the **Fonó Music Club**, Sztregova utca 3; tel: 206-5300; <www.fono.hu>. Take tram No. 47 from Móricz Zsigmond körtér to Kalotaszeg utca. *Táncház* is mostly performed during the winter months but there are summer festivals; check with Tourinform if you are interested; <www.tanchaz.hu> also has information.

Nocturnal jazz

Two clubs to try are: **Kalamajka Táncház** (Arany János utca 10, tel: 354-3400; open Sat 5pm–2am) and **Csángó Dance House** (Marczibányi tér 5/a, near the Moszkva tér metro; tel: 212-5789).

One well-known professional group is **Muzsikás**, which featured in the soundtrack for the film *The English Patient*. They make occasional appearances in Budapest, especially during the Spring Festival.

You can see Hungarian dancers, both amateur and professional, most nights at the Municipal Folklore Center, Fehérvári út 47, south of Gellért Hill. The **Hungarian**

State Folklore Ensemble, the **Danube Folklore Ensemble** and the **Rajkó Folk Ensemble** are established and excellent performers. They perform at the Budai Vigadó (Corvin tér 8), Duna Palota (Zrinyi utca 5), and the Bábszinház (Andrássy út 69); check <www.hungariakoncert.hu> for details.

Clubs and Bars

Look for the sign *söröző* if you are a beer drinker, and *borozó* if you prefer wine. While a *söröző* is often similar to a German *Bierstube*, a *borozó* is rarely like a Parisian wine bar. They do not exclusively serve beer or wine, either.

Expats and affluent local people go to **Becketts** (Bajcsy-Zsilinszky út 72), where they wait for Godot beneath a portrait of Samuel and posters advertising his plays. The bar sells 14 draught beers, including Guinness, and serve fish and chips, beef cooked in Guinness, and Irish breakfasts. There is music, and video links to major sporting events. The **Irish Cat** at Múzeum körút 41 is a cellar which also has a lot of Guinness and Kilkenny beer.

Fat Mo's Music Club and Speakeasy (Nyáry Pál utca 11) is a music venue with bar/restaurant that features jazz, soul, blues and regular DJ sets. They also do a cheap lunch.

Belgian beer-lovers will enjoy the **Belgian Brasserie** (Bem rakpart 12) where *moules frites* may be had with the beer.

The **Old Man's Music Pub** (Akácfa utca 13) hosts a wide range of rock, blues and jazz performances for occasionally rowdy fans. The place is smoky and a bit ramshackle, but crowded and friendly.

Real Hungarian pubs are rare in the central area, but **Bécsi söröző** (Papnövelde utca 8), near Ferenciek tere, is one, with lots of Ferencváros football club memorabilia.

If you wish to become more closely acquainted with Hungarian beer, **Dreher** have a beer museum – **Dreher sör múzeum** (Jászberényi utca 7–11; open daily 10am–6pm).

CHILDREN'S BUDAPEST

There are lots of things for children to do in Budapest. First stop, in fine weather, could be to hire a family-sized pedal car in City Park. At Vajdahunyad castle, there's summer boating and winter skating on the lake. Nearby are the Zoo and Vidámpark, a splendid old-fashioned fun-fair *(see page 69)*. Népliget Park has a Planetarium, which stages sound-and-light shows (open Mon–Sat 7.30pm; tel: 263-0871). There's a play area beside the Feneketlen tó (Bottomless Lake), which is home to ducks, fish, ringed snakes and tortoises. The Transport Museum, Rail Heritage Park, Children's Railway and chairlift in the Buda Hills are also all popular *(see pages 71, 76 and 44–5)*.

If the weather is bad, head for the Campona Centre (Nagytétényi út 37–45; bus from Gellért tér). It has a Peter Pan Playhouse and a Tropicarium with fish, insects, snakes, birds and small mammals. The Natural History Museum (Ludovika tér 2; open Wed–Mon 10am–6pm) offers hands-on exhibitions. The Palace of Miracles (Fény utca 20–22; open Mon–Fri 9am–6pm, Sat–Sun 9am–7pm) is an interactive scientific playhouse with over 100 games and experiments. The Puppet Theatre (Bábszinház; Andrássy út 69) has morning and matineé performances for children.

Making friends at the zoo

There's an ice-rink (Jégpálya) at the Pólus Centre XV (Szentmihályi út 131; open 9am–9pm; bus from Keleti pu); and roller-blades and skateboards are provided at Görzenál Skatepark, Árpád fejedelem utca. Eurocenter Gokart Pálya have an indoor karting track at Bécsi út 154.

Calendar of Events

Dates of events and festivals appear in *Where Budapest?* and other bulletins, and can be obtained from Tourinform and IBUSZ offices.

February. Filmszemle: a 10-day event during which new Hungarian films are screened at the Budapest Convention Centre. Opera Ball: at the Hungarian State Opera House.

March. Budapest Spring Festival: two weeks of the best in Hungarian music, theatre, dance and art. Spring Days: historical dramas enacted at Szentendre.

May. Book Week (end of May): a carnival atmosphere prevails as bookstalls sprout up all over Budapest selling the new season's books.

June. Summer concert season: Budapest's open-air cinemas begin their screenings, and theatres stage light drama, musicals, opera, operetta and revues. Danube Flower Carnival: (second week in June). Ferencváros Summer Festival. Jewish Summer Festival. Danube Water Carnival (mid-June): the anniversary of the founding of the Chain Bridge is celebrated with fireworks and aquatic events.

July. Summer concert season continues. Sziget Festival: (end July–August) on Óbuda Island. It's claimed to be Europe's biggest rock and pop festival.

August. St Stephen's Day: (20th) processions, Craftsmen's Fair in the Castle District, and firework display on Gellért Hill. Budafest: celebration of opera and ballet in the State Opera House. Wine Harvest Celebration: popular wine festival in Boglárlelle near Lake Balaton. Hungarian Grand Prix: Formula 1 cars race at the Hungaroring circuit. National Jewish Festival: music and art with Jewish themes.

September. Budapest International Wine Festival: wine-tasting stalls at Vörösmarty tér, festivities and parade. Wine harvest: Badacsony on Lake Balaton.

September/October. Autumn Festival, Budapest Arts Weeks: music, theatre, dance, and fine arts events take place at venues around the city, with renowned participants from all over the world.

EATING OUT

Magyar cuisine has a long history, but is little known outside Hungary. Traditionally, the nomadic Magyars cooked their food in a cauldron over an open fire, and traces of this kind of one-pot cooking can still be found in the hearty soups and cabbage-based dishes that crop up on many menus today. In the 17th century paprika arrived in the country; some say the Slavs or the Turks brought it, others say it came from the Americas. Paprika is a relatively mild seasoning, which should not be confused with the far hotter chilli. Hungarian food may be cooked in lard or goose fat, giving a heavier consistency and a richer taste than many Westerners are accustomed to. If restaurant portions are too hefty for you, order soup and then an appetiser instead of a main course. Some restaurants do small portions.

Paprika, Hungary's 'red gold'

Budapest has not always been noted for adventurous cooking but things have changed recently. There are chefs working in the city today who specialise in a variety of different styles and have brought an innovative 21st-century touch to old recipes that make them far more inviting.

Where to Eat

You won't often see the sign 'restaurant' in Budapest; when you do, the establishment is likely to cater to foreign tourists. The two most common names for a place to eat are *étterem* and *vendéglő*. A *csárda* (pronounced *chard-a*) is usually a country-style inn with a cosy atmosphere. Budapest has long rivalled Vienna for its café culture and love of pastries and coffee. Many cafés (*kávéház* and *cukrászda*) serve full meals as well as cakes.

When to Eat

Breakfast (*reggeli*) is generally served 7–10am. Hungarians don't eat much at the start of the day, but at most hotels a basic international breakfast buffet is served. Lunch (*ebéd*), generally served 1–3pm, is the main meal of the day, a fact reflected in the quantities that tend to be served. Dinner (*vacsora*) is served 7–10pm, although Hungarians in general are not late eaters.

What to Eat

Starters (*előételek*): Goose-liver paté and *hideg libamáj*, cold slices of goose liver served in its own fat on toast with purple onion rings, are perennial Hungarian favourites (the latter is also served as a main course). Pancakes (*palacsinta*) Hortobágy-style are filled with minced meat, deep-fried until crispy, and dressed with sour cream. Budapest is also a good place to try caviar (*kaviár*). The best is often Caspian.

Soups (*leves*): Soups are immensely popular and always on the menu. The well-known *gulyásleves* (goulash soup) is the standard bearer: chunks of beef, potatoes, onions, tomatoes and peppers are cooked with paprika, garlic and caraway for added flavour. Fishermen's soup (*halászlé*) is also based on potatoes, onions, tomatoes and paprika, with the addition of chunks of fresh-water fish. Also popular – and actually a meal in itself – is *babgulyás*, goulash soup served with dried beans. If you prefer a lighter soup, try consommé with quail eggs *(eroleves fürjtojással)*. You're also likely to find garlic cream soup served in a hollowed-out loaf.

Perhaps the most intriguing soup of all is *hideg meggyleves* (cold sour-cherry soup). Topped with frothy whipped cream, it would certainly be classified as a dessert elsewhere. On a hot day, try *hideg almaleves* – a creamy, refreshing cold apple soup, served with a dash of cinnamon.

Meat *(húsételek)*: Hungary is a nation of avid carnivores. *Pörkölt* is the stew that most closely approximates the West's notion of goulash. It can be made with beef, chicken or pork. *Maharpörkölt* is beef stew and *borjúpörkölt* is veal stew; the list is as long as the meats available. Veal and pork are the top choice of most Hungarians, whether fried, stewed or stuffed with combinations of ham, cheese, mushrooms or asparagus. Steaks, too, are usually on the menu. *Lecsó* is steak accompanied by a stew of peppers, tomatoes and onions. *Töltött káposzta* is another classic: cabbage leaves stuffed with pork and rice, served over sauerkraut with spicy sausage, paprika and a fattening dollop of sour cream.

Game and fowl: Game is very popular. Wild boar *(vaddisznó)* and venison *(oz)* frequently appear on menus, often reasonably priced. Chicken *(csirke)* is popular and inexpensive, and *csirke-paprikás* – chicken stewed with onions, green peppers, tomatoes, sour cream and paprika – ranks as something of a national dish. Goose is another favourite, prized for its flesh as well as its liver. Turkey often comes stewed or in stuffed portions,

> Hungarians love *lángos*, which is deep-fried batter, made more enticing by spreading it with garlic, cheese and sour cream. There are stands serving *lángos* at markets across Budapest.

Preparing fish in the traditional way

Kiev-style (with garlic butter) or with ham and cheese. Look out, too, for stag, hare, pheasant and wild duck.

Fish *(halételek)*: Local fish in this land-locked country is necessarily of the fresh-water variety; *ponty* (carp) and *fogas* (pike-perch from Lake Balaton) are the two most commonly found in Budapest, but they are somewhat bland. A tasty fish soup, served with paprika, is *halászlé*.

Vegetables and pasta: Vegan and vegetarian restaurants can be found, and vegetarian dishes increasingly appear on Hungarian menus. Vegetable accompaniments sometimes have to be ordered separately and can be uninspired. In some establishments you can get a fine Caesar or Greek salad but in others *saláta* may be little more than a plate of cabbage and pickled beetroot. What most Westerners call a mixed salad usually appears as *vitamin saláta*. Strict vegetarians will need to monitor the menu closely: classic dishes of stuffed pepper *(töltött paprika)* and stuffed cabbage *(töltött káposz-*

Tables at Fishermen's Bastion

ta) include pork in the filling, and many vegetable soups may include some meat or meat stock.

Dishes are usually served with boiled potatoes or with pasta, either in ribbon noodles *(nokedli)* or in the form of starchy dumplings *(galuska)*, often translated as gnocchi on the menu.

Desserts *(tészták)*: Hungarians love pastries and sweets, and two desserts are ubiquitous. One is the decadent Gundel pancake *(Gundel palacsinta)*, named after Hungary's most famous restaurateur. It is filled with nut and raisin paste, drenched in chocolate and sometimes flambéed. The equally calorific *somlói galuska* is a heavy sponge with vanilla, nuts, chocolate and whipped cream in an orange and rum sauce. Strudels *(rétes)* often have fruit and poppy-seed fillings. For simpler tastes, there is ice cream *(fagylalt)*, cheese *(sajt)* or fruit *(gyümölcs)*.

Drinks

Hungarian wines: The Great Plain, in southern Hungary, produces a wide range of wines, from vigorous and full-bodied reds to dry, smoky whites. The most famous of the white wines is Tokay (Tokaj), a rich, aged dessert wine. The grapes that produce this world-renowned wine are grown in the volcanic soil of the Tokay region in the northeast of Hungary. The grapes are left on the vine until autumn mists encourage the growth of the noble rot that gives the wine its intense sweetness and complex character. Tokay has been produced for over 200 years, and was a favourite of Catherine the Great and Louis XIV; it also inspired poetry from Voltaire and music from Schubert. Tokaji Furmint is dry, Tokaji Szamorodni is medium-sweet, akin to sherry, and Tokaji Aszú is full-bodied and sweet.

Less celebrated but perfectly satisfying white table wines come from the Lake Balaton region, including Riesling, Sauvignon Blanc and Chardonnay. Badacsonyi wines are the best known and have been enjoyed for some 2,000 years. Some of the best white wines in the country come from the smallest wine-producing region, Somló.

The Villány region produces some of Hungary's best reds, many of which are aged in oak casks, including the fine Villányi burgundi and the tannic Kékoportó. The best-known Hungarian red, which comes from the northeastern region, is the splendidly named Egri Bikavér (Bull's Blood of Eger) – a full-bodied and spicy accompaniment to meat or game dishes. More subtle is the Pinot Noir from the same town.

In the Clink

It's probably better not to clink glasses when drinking a toast. It is said that in 1849, when the Austrians executed 13 Hungarian revolutionaries, they were drinking, cheering and clinking glasses between each execution. Since then, many Hungarians have felt that it was insensitive to clink glasses. However, as the year 1999 approached, there were stories that the 'curse' was to run for only 150 years and then cease, so glasses may now be clinked in toasts. To avoid mistakes, its best to take your lead from the company you're in.

Maturing Hungarian reds

Beer *(sör)*: Hungarian beers go well with heavy, spicy foods. Except at the most formal restaurants, beer is as acceptable as wine to accompany a meal.

Other drinks: There are no recognised Hungarian apéritifs, but a Puszta cocktail – a mixture of apricot brandy, local cognac-style brandy, and sweet Tokay wine – is as good a way as any to start the evening.

Finish off your evening with one of Hungary's famous fruit brandies *(pálinka)*. They are fermented from the fruit and therefore have a clean, dry taste. The favourite is *barack* (apricot), followed by *cseresznye* (cherry). The country's national drink, the peculiar green herbal liqueur called Zwack Unicum, has been drunk for centuries.

Coffee *(kávé)*: This is a favourite Budapest drink, and it is most commonly served black, hot and sweet, espresso-style in thimble-sized cups. There used to be no alternative but now you'll find milk available everywhere, and cappuccino is served all over Budapest and in other large towns. Tea is also widely available, and a request for a pot of Earl Grey, or any other familiar type of tea, with lemon or milk, will raise no eyebrows in the city's better coffee houses.

To Help You Order

Waiter!	**Pincér!**
Menu.	**Étlap.**
Enjoy your meal.	**Jó étvágyat.**
The bill, please.	**Kérem a számlát.**
I'd like (an/some)…	**Kérek szépen…**

Menu Reader

alma	apple	**kacsa**	duck
ásvány víz	mineral water	**leves(ek)**	soup
		liba	goose
bab	beans	**marha**	beef
bárány	lamb	**paradiscom**	tomato
borjú	veal	**pisztráng**	trout
csípos	hot (spicy)	**ponty**	carp
csirke	chicken	**pörkölt**	stew
fehér bor	white wine	**ránsott sajt**	fried cheese
fogas	pike-perch	**sajt**	cheese
fózött	boiled	**saláták**	salad
gomba	mushroom	**sertés**	pork
gulyás	goulash	**sör**	beer
gyümölc	fruit	**sútve**	baked/fried
hagyma	onion	**tea**	tea
halak	fish	**tonhal**	tuna
halászlé	fish stew	**vad**	game
húsételek	meat dishes	**vajat**	butter
káposzta	cabbage	**víz**	water
kávé	coffee	**vörös bor**	red wine
kenyér	bread	**zöldság**	vegetables

HANDY TRAVEL TIPS

An A–Z Summary of Practical Information

A

ACCOMMODATION

Hotels in Budapest are graded from one star to five stars, and those rating three to five are of comparable international standard. The well-known international hotel chains are present, with prices about the same as anywhere else in Europe. Specialist hotels offer 'health and wellness' packages or sport and equestrian activity holidays.

There are some new hotels and hostels. The best low-budget option is to stay in a *panzió* (pension/bed-and-breakfast hotel). Many are set in the suburbs or the Buda Hills with the added advantage of serenity, greenery and great views. Self-catering apartments and rooms in private homes are a growing sector. IBUSZ and Tourinform offices can give you the addresses. Tourinform offices (including the one at the airport) have a comprehensive list of all hotels in Hungary, but only the IBUSZ offices at Vörösmarty tér 6; tel: 317-0532, and at Keleti and Nyugati railway stations, provide a booking service. Accommodation in private homes is well established in the Lake Balaton area, as the numerous German *Zimmer frei* (vacant room) signs indicate. Campsites are plentiful in Hungary, and there are eight in the environs of Budapest. It may come as a surprise, but many Hungarian hotels accept pets.

It is essential to book ahead during peak season (April to October). Rates are sky-high during the Hungarian Grand Prix in August. In order to be comfortable in July or August, make sure

I'd like a single room/double room.	**Egyágyas/Kétágyas szobát/kérek.**
with bath/with shower	**fürdő szobával/ zuhanyozó val**
What's the daily rate?	**Mibe kerül naponta?**

the room is equipped with air conditioning. Hotels generally quote prices in euros.

AIRPORT

Non-budget international flights arrive and depart from **Budapest Ferihegy Airport 2**, and budget airlines arrive and depart from **Ferihegy 1**, both 38km (24 miles) east of the capital. Terminal A is used by Malév (the Hungarian national airline) and Terminal B by all other airlines. Both terminals have car-hire agencies, money exchange desks, ATM machines and information offices.

It takes about 45 minutes to get from the airport to the centre of Budapest. The efficient **Airport Minibus** (tel: 296-8555) is the best deal; it is a shared taxi that will deliver you to and collect you from any address in Budapest (HUF 2,300 one-way, HUF 3,900 return). Look for the prominent 'Airport Minibus' sign at the information desk. Service is faster if you want to go to one of the big inner-city hotels, as there will be more passengers going to the same destination. There may be a slight wait if you wish to go off the beaten track. For the return journey, call 24 hours in advance to book. Your hotel will do this for you. Allow plenty of extra time – as much as an additional hour – in case of delays.

There is also a **public airport bus** (BKV Plusz Reptér busz). This is cheaper and deposits passengers at the Kőbánya-Kispest metro station.

If you want to take a taxi, there are vast numbers of them parked just off the road, outside the airport boundaries, waiting for radio calls from their offices. Once a call is received, the taxi will be with you in minutes. Avoid the touts looking for custom. The reputable companies are available at the terminal (Budataxi, Fő taxi, Rádiótaxi, Tele 5, 6x6 Taxi, Taxi 2000, etc). Always try to clarify the rate before setting out.

Airport information: tel: 296-9696.
Flight information: tel: 296-6000.

B

BUDAPEST CARD

The Budapest Card (Budapest Kártya) allows the holder (plus child aged under 14) 48 or 72 hours' travel and sightseeing. A booklet comes with the card, detailing all the services available. These include free travel on public transport; free admission to museums and many attractions; and discounts at restaurants, shops, the airport minibus, car hire and on tickets for cultural programmes and sightseeing tours. The card costs HUF 4,700 for 48 hours and HUF 5,900 for 72 hours. It is available from the airport, Tourinform, hotels, metro stations, etc.

BUDGETING FOR YOUR TRIP

Visitors expecting the dirt-cheap Central Europe of the past may be in for a shock. Budapest hotels are now on a par with those in Western Europe. However, many facets of daily life remain true bargains for visitors, including the highly efficient public-transport system, supermarket shopping, hearty food and drink, museum entrance fees and concert performances.

Transport to Budapest. Since May 2004, when Hungary joined the EU, a number of budget airlines have been running services from various European cities. Good deals combining travel and accommodation are available, too. Non-Europeans can expect their flights to eat up considerably more of their budgets, although it is worth looking for deals on the internet: you can sometimes fly to another European airport and complete the journey on a budget airline. Only Malév have direct flights from North America, so most US passengers will have to get a connecting flight anyway.

Local transport (*see also pages 124–5*). Public transport is very inexpensive. A single trip on a bus, tram or the metro costs just HUF 170 . Taxis are relatively expensive. Opt for public transport whenever possible and always phone for a taxi, if you really need one, rather than hailing one in the street.

Incidentals. Museum admission: HUF 100–900. Entertainment: tickets for theatre, musicals and classical music concerts range from HUF 700–4,000, although certain performances at the Hungarian Opera House can cost up to HUF 8,000. Excursions and tours: walking and city tours range from HUF 2,400–7,500, and Danube or Balaton trips from HUF 17,500–21,000.

C

CAR HIRE

Arrangements and conditions for car hire are similar to those in other European countries. The minimum age requirement is 21 years and you must have been in possession of a valid licence for at least 12 months. It is best to book in advance.

Rates for 1–3 days vary (upwards from HUF 15,000) for an economy-size car. Always ask if CDW (collision damage waiver) insurance is included in the price. Unleaded petrol costs HUF 290 per litre. Local agencies, such as **Budget Hungary** (tel: 214-0420; discount with Budapest Card) are the cheapest. The major agencies have offices at the airport and in Pest. Various firms' brochures are available from hotel reception desks and from Tourinform.

CLIMATE

Budapest is very cold in winter and swelters in sticky July and August. The best weather, and the best time to visit, is from May to early June and September to October.

The chart below shows Budapest's average daytime temperature in degrees centigrade and fahrenheit:

	J	F	M	A	M	J	J	A	S	O	N	D
°C	-2	0	6	12	16	20	22	21	17	11	6	1
°F	29	32	42	53	61	68	72	70	63	52	42	34

CLOTHING

Dress is indistinguishable from that in any other European capital: very few people wear traditional costume, except on special occasions. Dress smartly in casinos and restaurants.

CRIME AND SAFETY

Budapest has a low rate of violent crime, but use your common sense, don't take risks and be wary of pickpockets. Watch your belongings, especially on the metro or in crowded places. It's wise to make photocopies of travel documents and keep them in a separate place, such as a hotel safe.

Report any theft to the Tourist Police office (Vigadó út 6; 24 hours) and get a copy of your statement for your own insurance purposes. The emergency services phone number is 112.

CUSTOMS AND ENTRY REQUIREMENTS

Most visitors require a valid passport to enter Hungary. Since joining the EU, citizens of some European countries (France, Germany, Spain, Italy and a few others) require only an ID card. Citizens of many non-European countries do not need visas either. The Ministry of Foreign Affairs maintains a helpful and up-to-the minute website reporting requirements and changes (<www.mfa.gov.hu>). Those who need visas may obtain them from the Hungarian Consulate in their country of residence. There are single-, double- and multiple-entrance visas.

The Hungarian Customs and Finance Guard also maintains a homepage (<www.vam.hu>) giving details of regulations. Unlicensed weapons, pornography and drugs may not be imported. Travellers may bring 250 cigarettes, a litre of spirits and two litres of wine. EU regulations apply to citizens of member states.

Value-added tax, or VAT (known as ÁFA in Hungary), can be reclaimed on goods costing more than HUF 50,000. Shops participating in the scheme are responsible for making the refund to travellers who are entitled to it. For information on refunds, contact Global Refund Tax-Free Shopping Ltd (Global Refund Magyaroszág Kft; II Bég utca 3–5, tel/fax: 212-4906, <www.globalrefund.com>).

Currency restrictions. There have been no restrictions since June 2000, although the export and import of large amounts – HUF 200,000 or more – should be declared.

D

DRIVING

To take your car into Hungary you need a valid driving licence and car registration papers. Cars from most European countries are presumed to be fully insured, so no extra documentation need be shown. To be on the safe side, carry proof of insurance.

Road conditions. Hungary has one of the highest accident rates in Europe, and Budapest drivers are notorious for their recklessness. Central Budapest boulevards are many lanes wide and you have to contend with trams and trolley buses as well as heavy traffic.

Hungary's expanding motorway system is well-maintained and expanding. A toll sticker is required for most sections of the Hungarian motorways. These cost HUF 35,000 for a year; HUF 3,900 for a month; HUF 2,300 for 10 days and HUF 1,460 for four days. Stickers can be bought at toll booths, service stations along the motorway and the Hegyeshalom border crossing. Yellow emergency telephones are spaced every 2km (1¼ miles) along motorways M1, M5 and M7, and along the No. 5 highway.

Rules and regulations. These are based on the Vienna and Geneva conventions, so general international regulations apply. Drive on the right and pass on the left, but be careful at all times. Cars must be fitted with a nationality plate or sticker. A set of spare bulbs, a first-aid kit, and a warning triangle are also obligatory. Seatbelts are compulsory in front and back seats; children under 12 are prohibited from travelling in the front seat. Motorcycle riders and passengers must wear crash helmets. Using a hand-held mobile phone while driving is prohibited. Don't drink and drive: any amount of alcohol in the bloodstream is a punishable offence.

Speed limits. These are 130km/h (80mph) on motorways, 110 km/h (68mph) on highways, 90 km/h (55mph) on major roads, and 50km/h (31mph) in built-up areas, with on-the-spot fines for speeding. In resorts and built-up areas where there are lots of children, a 30km/h (18mph) speed limit may be imposed. Look for signs.

Fuel *(benzin)*. Petrol stations are frequent along highways and main roads, but don't venture down minor roads without filling up. Stations are usually open 6am–10pm; there is 24-hour service in the populated areas. Unleaded fuel is widely available (about HUF 290 a litre). You can usually pay for petrol with a credit card. If an attendant fills your car, you should give them a small tip.

Parking. There are meters (HUF 100–300), and public car parks. Try to find a hotel with a car park, leave your car there and take the metro. A car parked in a prohibited zone will be towed away or clamped.

If you need help. Remember to put out a red warning triangle 50m (165ft) behind your car. In the event of an accident, call the police. (tel: 107). This is compulsory if anyone is injured, and even if there are no injuries, there may be claims for damage or other consequences. If matters are serious, foreign citizens have a right to an interpreter and a lawyer. Cars with damaged bodywork are allowed out of the country only if they have an official certificate for the damage. If the vehicle at fault has a Hungarian licence plate, claims for damages go to your own insurance company or to the Hungaria Biztositó RT (The Hungarian Insurance Company's Auto Insurance department at Galvani út 44; tel: 421-1421; open Mon–Fri 8am–8pm). If the accident was caused by a foreign vehicle, claims must be made to the Hungária Insurance Company.

Tel: 188 for help from the **Hungarian Automobile Club's Yellow Angels** anywhere in Hungary, day or night.

Road signs. International pictographs are in use in Hungary. Motorways are indicated by green signs, all other main roads by dark blue.

Full tank, please.	**Kérem, töltse tele a tankot.**
Check the oil/tyres/ battery, please.	**Kérem, ellenorizze az olal jat/ a gumikat/ az akkumulátort.**
I've broken down.	**Meghibásodott a kocsim.**
There's been an accident.	**Baleset történt.**
Can I park here?	**Szabad itt parkolnom?**

E

ELECTRICITY

The current is 220 volts throughout Hungary. Take a two-pin adapter as necessary.

EMBASSIES AND CONSULATES

Australia: XII Királyhágo tér 8–9; tel: 457-9777
Canada: XII Budakeszi út 32; tel: 275-1200
Ireland: V Szabadság tér 7 (in Bank Centre); tel: 302-9600
UK: V Harmincad utca 6; tel: 266-2888
US: V Szabadság tér 12; tel: 475-4400

EMERGENCIES

Emergency telephone numbers throughout Hungary are as follows:

General Emergency **112**
Ambulance **104**
Fire **105**
Police **107**

English-speaking 24-hour medical service, tel: 200-0100.

G

GAY AND LESBIAN TRAVELLERS

Budapest has an active gay community. There is a monthly gay listings magazine, *Mások* (*Others*), gay radio programmes and a monthly gay erotic magazine. However, Budapest's gays and lesbians are not yet wholly accepted by the mainstream community. The age of consent for gay sex is 18 in Hungary; consensual sexual contact between heterosexuals is allowed from the age of 14. A **gay hotline** (tel: 0630 932-3334, English and German spoken) and the website <gayguide.net/Europe/Hungary/Budapest> serves the gay community.

Gay hangouts include the **Király thermal baths** (especially Saturday afternoon) and the following nightspots – which are just a few of many: **Mystery Bar-klub**, V Nagysándor József utca 3; **Action Bar**, V Magyar utca 42; **Darling**, V Szép utca 1; **CoXx Men's Bar**, VIII Dohány utca 38; **Árkádia**, V Türr Istvan utca 5; and **Uniformis Klub**, XIII Radnótis Miklós utca 3.

GETTING THERE

Air travel. Since May 2004, when Hungary joined the EU, a number of budget airlines have opened new routes. EasyJet, SkyEurope, Air Berlin, WizzAir, germanwings, Snowflake, bmi and others now fly from various European cities. British Airways, Lufthansa, KLM, Czech Airlines etc also fly to Budapest. There are plenty of options and low fares. The Hungarian national airline, Malév, has flights from Heathrow, Gatwick and Stansted. The flying time from London to Budapest, is just over two hours. Malév flies direct to Budapest every day except Friday from New York (9–10 hours) and operates a partnership with Delta Airlines. Malév also flies non-stop from Toronto to Budapest every Tuesday (additional flights during summer months).

Rail travel. Budapest can be reached by train from any major European city, although there are no direct trains from the UK (options include travelling via Paris to Munich and then on to Budapest or via Dover to Ostend and Vienna). Either way the journey time is at least 24 hours. Check <www.raileurope.co.uk> for details. Unless you are aged under 26 or over 60, it's an expensive option, and even for those with age-related discounts it is not really cheap.

The following international rail passes are valid in Hungary: InterRail, Euro Domino, EurailPass (and its variants), European East Pass, and Hungarian FlexiPass. In the US tel: (800) 4 EURAIL. Budapest has three international railway stations, **Keleti**, **Nyugati** and **Déli** (all have metro stations attached).

By car/coach. Budapest is connected by major motorways to Berlin, Prague and Vienna. It has always been held that the cheapest way to get from London to Budapest is by coach, although with the advent of budget airlines, that may no longer be the case. The bus journey takes some 31 hours and may not be much fun in summer, as buses can get crowded. See <www.national express.com> for details.

Long-haul buses arrive at Népliget Coach Station (Üllői út 131; tel: 219-8080).

If you plan to drive across the continent, the most direct route is via Ostend, Brussels, Cologne, Frankfurt, Linz and Vienna. Budapest is about 1,730km (1,080 miles) from London.

GUIDES AND TOURS

There are numerous guided tours in Budapest: **Cityrama** (tel: 302-4382); **Budatours** (tel: 374-7050); **Barbiebus** (tel: 922-2111); TGV **Tours** (tel: 354-0755); **Program Centrum** (tel: 318-4446); IBUSZ (tel: 317-7767) and the curiously named **Queenybus** (tel: 247-7159) offer an assortment of services. Tickets for city tours range from HUF 5,500–9,000.

Tours are available to the Danube Bend, the Puszta, and Lake Balaton; as are special interest tours (health and wellness, seasonal customs and folklore, etc).

Mahart Passnave (tel: 318-1704), **Legenda KFT** (tel: 266-4190), and **Program Centrum** (tel: 318-4446) offer Danube boat trips. There are evening cruises with music and dancing. You can also go sightseeing by helicopter, light aircraft or hot-air balloon. Hotel reception areas have brochures about excursions and Tourinform can also help.

Walking tours of special interest include **Absolute Walking Tours** (tel: 211-8861; <www.absolutetours.com> and **Paul Street Tours** (tel: 06 20 933-5240; <www.firsteuropeanshipping.com>).In season, the Municipality of Budapest organise twice-daily tours: 'Royal Legends' and 'Secrets of Buda Castle'. Tickets and information from Buda Castle Information office, Tárnok utca 15, tel: 488-0453. **Robinson Tours**, tel: 486-3670, offer highlights of the city. Tours of Jewish Budapest are conducted by **Chosen Tours**, tel: 355-2202 and the Municipality of Budapest also leads **Jewish Heritage** walking tours, tel: 317-2754. Audio-tape guides are available for hire at the National Museum and the Open Air Village Museum near Szentendre.

Yellow Zebra Bike Tours, tel: 266-8777, leave Deák tér May–Oct daily 11am; additional 3pm departure July–Aug. The company provides the essentials.

There is also a new initiative, **Budapest-riksa**, tel: 06 30 951-5916; <www.riksa.hu>, which rents out rickshaws.

H

HEALTH AND MEDICAL CARE

Hungarian doctors and health-care professionals are highly skilled, and most speak English and German. The Hungarian National Health Service is well-equipped to handle emergencies and there are reciprocal arrangements for citizens of the EEA (European Economic Area) which includes the EU member countries plus Norway, Iceland and Liechtenstein. Emergency treatment is free for foreigners; all other treatment has to be paid for when you receive the service, so it is vital that you take out private health insurance.

The **American Clinic** is located in district I, Hattyú utca 14; tel: 224-9090. For 24-hour medical care, call **Főnix SOS Rt** (XII, Diós árok 1–3; tel: 200-0100), which has an ambulance service.

Tap water is drinkable, but don't drink anything marked *nem ivóviz*, which means non-drinkable.

Where's the nearest pharmacy?	**Hol a legközelebbi patika?**
I need a doctor/dentist.	**Orvosra/Fogorvosra van szük ségem.**

Pharmacies. Look for the sign *gyógyszertár* or *patika*. Chemists only sell pharmaceutical and related products. For cosmetics and toiletries you will need an *illatszerbolt* or *drogéria*; for photo supplies a *fotószaküzlet*. The *Budapest Sun* and Tourinform carry lists of night pharmacies. Among them are **Teréz Patika**, VI Teréz körút 41; tel: 311-4439; and II Frankel Leo utca 22; tel: 212-4406.

HOLIDAYS *(hivatalos ünnep)*

1 January	New Year's Day
15 March	National Holiday Anniversary of 1848 Revolution)
April	Easter Monday

1 May	Labour Day
June	Pentecost
20 August	St Stephen's Day
23 October	Remembrance (Republic) Day
25 December	Christmas Day
26 December	Boxing Day

I

INTERNET

There are many internet cafes. The following is just a selection:

Ami, V Váci utca 40; tel: 267-1644; daily 9am–midnight.

Cyber Net, Café Eckermann; VI Andrássy út 24; tel: 269-2542; Mon–Fri 8am–10pm, Sat 9am–10pm. Offers free internet use once a week on three terminals, but there's a waiting list, so sign up around four days in advance.

Vista Kávéház, Paulay Ede utca 7; tel: 268-0888; Mon–Fri 10am–10pm, Sat 10am–8pm.

L

LANGUAGE

Hungarian is the mother tongue of 95 percent of the population. It is wholly unrelated to the languages of the surrounding countries and is classified in the Finno-Ugric family of languages. It is notoriously difficult and continues to baffle linguists. Many Budapestis speak German, and many, especially the young, speak English fluently.

One source of confusion is how to address a Hungarian. The surname always precedes the Christian name; Western Europeans would say or write Károly Jókai, whereas Hungarians say Jókai Károly. Second, there is no direct equivalent of Mr or Mrs; the nearest terms, which are very formal, are *Uram* for Mr and *Hölgyem* for Mrs. You can mix East and West by saying, for example, Mr Jókai.

Yes/no	**igen/nem**
please	**kérem**
Good morning	**Jó reggelt**
Good afternoon	**Jó napot**
Goodnight	**Jó éjszakát**
Goodbye	**Viszontlátásra**
Thank you	**Köszönöm**

Do you speak English/
    French/German?
	**Beszél angolul/
	    franciául/németül?**

entrance/exit	**bejárat/kijárat**
pull/push	**húzni/tolni**
open/closed	**nyitva/zárva**
Good day (formal)	**Tó napot**
Hi (informal, singular/plural)	**Szia/Sziasztok**
open	**nyitva**
closed	**zárva**
entrance	**bejárat**
exit	**kijárat**
road	**út**
street	**utca**
square	**tér**
boulevard	**körút**
bridge	**híd**
pharmacy	**gyógyszertár**
post office	**posta**
railway station	**pályaudvar**
shop	**bolt/üzlet**
department store	**áruház**

LEFT LUGGAGE

There are facilities at the three main railway stations and at the Central Bus Station.

M

MAPS

Both Tourinform and IBUSZ offices supply visitors with free maps of the city that are sufficient for most purposes. You should also pick up a Budapest Transport Authority map *(BKV térkép)*, available free at metro stations. If you want a more comprehensive map, look for the *Cartographia Budapest City* or *Budapest Atlas* maps of Budapest, available in bookstores. For an interactive map of the city, visit <www.fsz.bme.hu/hungary/budapest/cgi-bin/search_tkp>.

MEDIA

Newspapers and magazines. Two English-language weekly newspapers are the *Budapest Sun*, which features an excellent 'What's On' section and *Budapest Business Journal*. *Budapest Week* is a younger, more lively publication with features and listings. Major European and US newspapers usually arrive on the day of publication, although some are a day late. *Where Budapest?* (in English) is the essential monthly magazine for finding out what's on. It is free and available through hotels and tourist information offices. *Pesti Est* has comprehensive listings of nightlife activities. It isn't in English, but listings are usually more or less decipherable, as performers' names and venues are straightforward. Many of these publications are now on-line.

Radio and television. English news can be heard on the hour between 5am and 10pm at Radio Bridge (FM102.1 MHz). All hotels rated 4-star and above, and some 3-star, offer satellite television.

MONEY

Currency. The unit of currency is the forint (HUF). Coins in circulation are HUF 1, 2, 5, 10, 20, 50 and 100. Banknotes come in denominations of HUF 100, 200, 500, 1,000, 2,000, 5,000, 10,000 and 20,000.

Foreign exchange offices. These are found in banks, hotels, larger campsites, travel agents and large shops, but some offer exchange rates as much as 20 percent lower than banks, which always offer the most advantageous rates. There isn't a black market any more, so if you are accosted and offered money-changing opportunities, steer clear. It's good to have a few dollars, euros or pounds for emergencies, and you may get a better rate of exchange for cash.

Credit and debit cards. Visa, MasterCard, AmEx, Cirrus, etc, are frequently accepted in hotels, restaurants and large shops (look for the logos). Supermarkets, museums, and railway stations expect payment in cash. Post offices (there are more than 3,200 of them) will dispense cash on production of your card.

ATMs. Cash machines are widespread and most major cards are accepted. They dispense HUFs.

Travellers cheques. These may be cashed at banks, hotels, etc., and may sometimes be used in place of cash, although you will almost certainly get a poorer rate of exchange than if you convert them to cash. Commission is generally charged.

O

OPENING HOURS

Most businesses in Budapest are open Mon–Fri 8am–5pm. **Shopping centres** are open Mon–Sat 10am–9pm, Sun 10am–6pm. Smaller **shops** are open Mon–Fri 9 or 10am–6 or 7pm, Sat 9 or 10am–1 or 2pm, but some close all day Saturday. For 24-hour shopping look for the sign 'Non-Stop'. **Banks** open Mon–Fri 8am–3pm, although some close at 1pm on Friday. **Museums** mostly open Tues–Sun 10am–6pm. **Post offices** *(see next page)* open Mon–Fri 8am–6pm, Sat 8am–1pm.

P

POLICE *(rendorség)*

Police wear blue-and-grey uniforms. Traffic police also wear white caps and white leather to make them more visible. During July and August, tourist police with translators patrol the streets.

Police: tel: 107
Budapest Police Headquarters: tel: 343-0034

Where is the nearest police station?	**Hol van a legközelebbi rendőrség?**

POST OFFICES

Post offices (Magyar Posta) handle mail, telephones, telegraphs, telex and (at the larger offices) fax. Stamps *(bélyeg)* are best bought at tobacconists or where postcards are sold. Most hotels will stamp and post your mail for you. Post boxes are painted red.

Most post offices open Mon–Fri 8am–6pm, Sat 8am–1pm. The offices near the two mainline stations open 8am–9pm. The one near Nyugati station is at Teréz körút 51–53; and that near Keleti station, Baross tér 11/c.

express (special delivery)	**expressz küldemény**
airmail	**légiposta**
I'd like a stamp for this letter/postcard please.	**Kérek egy bélyeget erre a levélre/a képeslapra.**

International postcards cost HUF 110 to Europe and HUF 130 to the US. Letters (20g) cost HUF 170 to Europe and HUF 190 to the US (correct at time of printing). DHL, Federal Express and UPS delivery services have offices in Budapest.

PUBLIC TRANSPORT

The Budapest Transport Authority (BKV) operates an extensive, cheap, clean and reliable system with three metro lines, blue local buses, yellow trams and red trolley-buses. Throughout central Budapest, you are never more than a few minutes' walk from a bus, tram or metro line, and waiting times are rarely more than a few minutes. Maps of the whole network are available from major metro and railway stations, Tourinform, etc. You must buy a ticket before boarding. They are sold at stations, travel bureaux and tobacconists. An HÉV suburban railway ticket costs HUF 94. A travel card is good value. A single ticket costs HUF 170, 10 cost HUF 1,450, 20 cost HUF 2,800. A day card costs HUF 1,350. If you are staying for several days, it makes sense to buy a three- or seven-day travel card at HUF 2,700 and HUF 3,100. Not only are they cheaper but they save the trouble of validating new tickets when changing trains, etc. Current fares and additional information are available at <www.bkv.hu>.

Most public transport runs between 4.30am and 11.30pm. There are a limited number of night buses and trams (look for the suffix é on their number). Don't forget to validate your ticket by punching it in the red machine (passes don't need validating), which are located onboard buses and trams, and for trains on line 1 of the metro. On metro lines 2 and 3 you have to use the orange machines just inside the station entrance. BKV ticket inspectors, wearing red armbands, patrol public transport frequently and they are extremely vigilant. Fare dodgers have to pay an on-the-spot fine.

Buses (*busz*). A bus stop is marked by a blue-bordered rectangular sign with the letter **M** and a list of stops on the route. Signal that you want to get off by pressing the bell.

Mini-buses. A convenient mini *várbusz* service runs an almost constant shuttle between Moszkva tér and Dísz tér (next to the funicular railway) on Castle Hill, stopping every 200m/yds.

Trams *(villamos)*. Yellow trams, usually of three to four carriages, cover a 190-km (120-mile) network; some run throughout the night. Tram No. 2 travels along the Danube Bank on the Pest side. Trams Nos 4 and 6 follow the Outer Ring (or Nagykörút) and Nos 47 and 49 follow Kiskörút, the Inner Ring.

Taxis *(taxi)*. Budapest's taxi drivers are notorious for overcharging foreigners, and unless you're laden with luggage or have some other reason for not travelling on public transport, they should be avoided. If, however, you do want a taxi, call one of the following firms: **Fő Taxi** (tel: 222-2222), **Radio Taxi** (tel: 377-7777), **Budataxi** (tel: 233-3333), **Tele5taxi** (tel: 355-5555), **Citytaxi** (tel: 211-1111) or **6x6 Taxi** (tel: 266-6666). Fares are variable and subject to change. Hailing a cab on the street is not recommended, but if you do so, always find out the rate and make sure the meter is working (and set at zero before you set off), or agree on the fare in advance.

Metro. The metro operates three lines. The only interchange between the lines is at Deák tér station. Remember you have to use a new ticket each time you change lines – a problem solved by buying a pass *(see page 124)*.

Coaches. Coaches to the airport, other parts of Hungary and European destinations run from Erzsébet tér station. Buses to the Danube Bend leave from Árpád station. For service information, tel: 485-2100.

Trains. There are three HÉV suburban commuter lines. Szentendre (via Aquincum) is reached via Batthyány tér station and Gödöllö is reached from Örs vezér tere. If you have a travel card, you pay only for the stretch outside Budapest city limits. Inter-city trains operate from three Budapest stations: **Keleti** (Baross tér; tel: 413-4610; most international trains), **Nyugati** (Nyugati tér; tel: 349-8503; mostly destinations east), and **Déli** (Alkotás u; tel: 375-6593).

The main MÁV **ticket office** for national and international trains is located at Andrássy út 35 (tel: 461-5400 or 461-5500).

A special treat for train enthusiasts are the **nostalgia trains**, vintage and steam locomotives run by MÁV Nosztalgia (tel: 238-0558 or 269-5242; <www.mavnosztalgia.hu>) that go to the Gödöllö Palace, the Hungarian Plain, Danube Bend, and Eger. The Royal Hungarian Express visits the cities of the old Austro-Hungarian Empire (Budapest, Prague and Vienna).

River transport. Pleasure boats run to and from the Danube Bend in the summer season (tel: 318-1223/484-4012). Hydrofoils also run to Esztergom and Vienna (tel: 484-4010).

R

RELIGION

The majority of Hungarians are Roman Catholics. Mass is usually said in Hungarian, but in some churches it is said in Latin, English or German. Other denominations and faiths, notably Protestant, Eastern Orthodox and Jewish, are also represented. There is a small number of Muslims.

Where Budapest? and the *Budapest Sun* both publish details of services in the city held in English and other languages.

T

TELEPHONES *(telefon)*

Phone cards may be purchased at newsstands, tobacconists, post offices, filling stations and supermarkets (including Tesco). Almost all public phones have a number so that people can call you back.

Local phone charges are quite cheap in Hungary. There are companies offering cheap calls and internet use: <www.neophone.hu>, <www.telecard.hu> and <www.micronet.hu>.

To make an international call from a public phone, dial the international access code (00), followed by the country code and the telephone number, including the area code. There are no off-peak rates. For national calls beyond Budapest, dial the national access code (06), followed by the area code and number. A local call within Budapest has 7 digits; it is not necessary to dial the area code. Mobile telephone numbers have 11 digits. The network is being modernised, so numbers change frequently. If the number has changed, there's a message in Hungarian followed by one in English (so don't hang up) giving the new number.

For international directory assistance, tel: 199.

TIME ZONES

Hungary follows Central European Time (Greenwich Mean Time +1 hour, or US Eastern Standard Time +6 hours). In summer the clock is put one hour ahead (GMT +2).

TIPPING

Tipping is the norm in Hungary. It is customary to leave 10–15 percent at restaurants and round up the bill in bars. Some restaurants may add a 10 percent service charge to the bill, so look carefully and ask, if this appears to be the case, so that you avoid tipping twice. Porters, hotel maids, toilet attendants, gypsy violinists playing at your table, masseurs at thermal baths and tourist guides also expect tips.

TOILETS

In Budapest all public toilets are pay toilets. Some cafés may even charge patrons for use of their facilities, others admit patrons free on production of a receipt for what they have consumed.

WC *(vay-tsay)*	toilet

For men's toilets, look out for the word *Férfiak* or, more commonly, *férfi* (occasionally *urak*). For women, look for *Nők* or (again, more commonly) *női* (and occasionally *hólgyek*).

TOURIST INFORMATION *(turista információs iroda)*

The main offices of **Tourinform**, the Hungarian Tourist Board, are V Vigadó utca 6 and Sütő utca 2 (near Deák tér metro station); tel: 317-9800; <www.hungarytourism.hu>). The Vigadó office is open 24 hours; the Sütő utca office, daily 8am–8pm. It also has an office in the Nyugati railway station; tel: 302-8580, and Tárnok utca 9–11 on Castle Hill; tel: 488-0453. Tourinform have numerous branches – they seem to be everwhere. The main **Tourism Office of Budapest** is located at VI Liszt Ferenc tér 11; tel: 322-4098; <www.budapestinfo.hu>. A 24-hour **tourist information hotline** is maintained on tel: 438-8080.

The main IBUSZ **office** is also at Sütő utca 2, 50m (165ft) from the Déak tér metro station. Another office is Ferenciek tere 10, tel: 485-2700. IBUSZ is also a major tour operator, providing a booking service and organising excursions. Opening hours are Mon–Fri 8am–5.30pm. There is a 24-hour IBUSZ branch at Petőfi tér 3; tel: 318-5707.

Hungarian National Tourist Board offices abroad:
UK: 46 Eaton Place, London SW1 X8AL, tel: (020) 7823-1055; fax: (020) 7823-1459.
US: 150 East 58th Street, New York, NY 10155, tel: (212) 355-0240; fax: (212) 207-4103, <www.gotohungary.com>.

TRAVELLERS WITH DISABILITIES

Budapest is improving access for travellers with disabilities. Currently, access ranges from excellent to non-existent. Public transport is difficult, but there are now buses equipped to take wheelchairs on some routes. Furthermore, there is a door-to-door taxi-like service which can be called upon (check the website <www.bkv.hu>). A few metro stations now have lifts and more are planned. Some museums are accessible. The spa hotels are fully equipped, and many larger hotels have some adapted rooms and wheelchair access.

W

WEBSITES

The following websites may be useful:

- <www.budapest.com>
- <www.budapestinfo.com>
- <www.budapestpanorama.com>
- <www.budapestsun.com>
- <www.budepesttimes.hu>
- <www.budapestweek.com>
- <www.gotohungary.com>
- <www.hungarytourism.hu>
- <www.kulturinfo.hu>
- <www.pestiside.hu>
- <www.visitorsguide.hu>

WEIGHTS AND MEASURES

Like the rest of continental Europe, Hungary uses the metric system.

YOUTH HOSTELS *(Ifjúsági szállás)*

There is an increasing number of hostels in Budapest. Avoid the touts at the railway station offering hostel accommodation. They will send you to somewhere expensive in the back of beyond. The International Youth Hostels Federation can be accessed at <www.hihostels.com>. You can also pick up a list of addresses at Tourinform or visit the Travellers' Youth Hostels information centre (tel: 343-0748; open daily 7am–8pm) at the Keleti railway station. Reports of the existing hostels are varied and contradictory, but what one person thinks is heaven may be another's idea of hell.

Recommended Hotels

Hotels in Hungary are graded from one to five stars. Budapest's standard visitor accommodation has improved in recent years, but choices are still limited, especially at the lower end of the range. It is always wise to book ahead, particularly for September, New Year, Easter, and the first or second weekend in August, when the Hungarian Grand Prix is staged. High season on Lake Balaton is from Easter to September, and during peak times demand is such that some establishments offer half-board only.

The following guide denotes the rack rate price of a double room with bath/shower in high season (May through October, as well as Christmas) including breakfast and VAT. Hotel room rates, especially at the upper end, are usually quoted in euros, though some are given in US dollars. All accept major credit cards, except where noted.

€€€€€	over 250 euros
€€€€	200–250 euros
€€€	150–200 euros
€€	100–150 euros
€	less than 100 euros

BUDA

Budapest art'otel €€–€€€ *I Bem rakpart 16–19, tel: 487-9487, fax: 487-9488, <www.artotel.hu>*. This is a chic hotel in high modernist style designed by Donald Sultan, the American contemporary artist, and it displays 600 of his works. The hotel is housed in four baroque townhouses beside the Danube, opposite Parliament. It's a hip, lifestyle hotel with a good restaurant, Chelsea, serving light, tasty meals. Wheelchair access. 165 rooms.

Carlton Hotel €–€€ *I Apor Péter utca 3, tel: 224-0999, fax: 224-0990, <www.carltonhotel.hu>*. A fairly modern building at the foot of Fishermen's Bastion in a quiet alleyway. Swiss owned, simply furnished and very clean. Some of the upper rooms have great views. Healthy breakfasts. 95 rooms.

Citadella € *XI Citadella sétány, tel: 466-5794, fax: 386-0505, <www.citadella.hu>*. Spartan but clean budget accommodation within the old castle boundaries on Gellért Hill. Some rooms have magnificent views. Coach invasions by day, tranquillity by night (unless student groups are resident). 12 rooms and one 14-bed dormitory.

Corinthia Aquincum €€–€€€€ *III Árpád Fejedlem útja 94, tel: 436-4100, fax: 436-4156, <www.corinthiahotels.com>*. Located near the Árpád Bridge, this is a modern, luxury, thermal-bath hotel that has recently been refurbished . Full spa and balneotherapy facilities. Attractive restaurants and bars and a newly established executive club for business travellers. Wheelchair access. 310 rooms.

Danubius Hotel Gellért €€€ *XI Gellért tér 1, tel: 889-5500, fax: 889-5505, <www.danubiusgroup.com/gellert>*. The famed Hotel Gellért faces the Liberty Bridge in Buda. Not a sleek modern box, but an art nouveau building of character. It has large rooms, antiques, splendid views and access to baths and pools plus medical and physiotherapy services. 234 rooms.

Hilton €€€€€ *Hess András tér 1–3, tel: 889-6600, fax: 889-6644, <www.hilton.com>*. One of the most luxurious hotels in town, with arguably the best location, on top of Castle Hill. You'll either love or hate the modern hotel's incorporation of a 13th-century Dominican church. The excellent facilities include a business centre and casino. The Dominican Restaurant overlooks Fishermen's Bastion and offers both light, healthy meals and dishes that are sheer indulgence. Wheelchair access. 322 rooms.

Hotel Victoria €–€€ *I Bem rakpart 11, tel: 457-8080, fax: 457-8088, <www.victoria.hu>*. This is a small, modern hotel facing the Danube on the Buda side. The rooms are spacious and the service is efficient and friendly. High-speed internet connection is available and there are laptops for hire. The price is excellent for the location. 27 rooms.

Kulturinnov € *I Szentháromság tér 6, tel: 355-0122, fax: 375-1886.* Tucked inside a handsome Renaissance building (the Hungarian Cultural Foundation) just steps from the Mátyás Church, this small hotel's location is unbeatable. Rooms are basic and small, unlike the grand central staircase and arches of the entrance, but a very good deal for the centre of Castle Hill. Difficult to get a room, but worth a try. 16 rooms.

Novotel Budapest Congress €€ *XII Alkotás utca 63–67, tel: 372-5700, fax: 466-5636, <www.novotel-bud-congress.hu>.* Modern hotel in a park area, surrounded by spreading chestnut trees. It's next door to the Budapest Convention Centre, so handy for events there. Two restaurants, one serving international and Hungarian fare and the other, the Bowling Brasserie, with four bowling lanes. Good value. 319 rooms.

MARGARET ISLAND

Danubius Thermal Hotel Margitsziget €€€ *XIII Margitsziget, tel: 889-4700, fax: 889-4988*; and **Danubius Grand Hotel Margitsziget** €€€ *XIII Margitsziget, tel: 452-6200, fax: 452-6262, <www.danubiusgroup.com>.* Contrasting hotels linked by a tunnel. The 'Grand Old Lady' of the island was built in 1893. The Thermal Hotel dates from 1979 and was the first city health resort. As well as an idyllic location, the hotels offer therapy for locomotive disorders, dentistry, cardiac and cosmetic surgery and a large range of health and beauty services. The hotels offer various packages. Naturally, there is provision for travellers with disabilities. 267 and 164 rooms respectively.

PEST

Amadeus Apartments € *V József Nádor tér 10, tel: 06 30 942-2893, fax: 302-8268, <www.amadeus.hu>.* Independent, fully equipped apartments, mostly in Pest, but also in Buda, ideal for those who like to come and go as they please and do their own cooking; 1–4 people can be accommodated in two-room apartments, each with bath, toilet and cooking facilities. Short-term lets.

6 apartments. Rent is about €15–30 per person per night, depending on size of apartment and number of guests.

Astoria €€–€€€ *V Kossuth Lajos utca 19, tel: 889-6000, fax: 889-6091, <www.danubiushotels.com>*. The Astoria is like a film set. It has tradition and style, with mirrors, chandeliers and carpets that evoke the ambience of the *belle époque*. It was given the name when it opened in 1914 by the first manager, who had been at the Waldorf Astoria in New York. It's been updated and is still a fine hotel. The Empire Restaurant serves fine Hungarian fare and the Café Mirror is worth a visit for the glittering decor. 135 rooms.

Budapest Marriott €€€€–€€€€€ *V Apáczai Csere János utca 4, tel: 266-7000, fax: 266-5000, <www.marriott.com/budhu>*. A newly renovated city centre hotel on the banks of the Danube. Every luxuriously appointed room enjoys splendid views of Castle Hill and many have small balconies. Friendly and efficient service and excellent facilities, including business and fitness centres. Wheelchair access. 362 rooms.

Domina Hotel Fiesta €€ *V Király utca 20, tel: 328-3000, fax: 266-6024, <www.domina.it/fiesta>*. Newish hotel in an historic building close to the basilica and synagogue. The hotel has four specially equipped rooms for guests with allergies and for disabled travellers. A dentist is also available on site. 112 rooms.

Erzsébet Hotel €€ *V Károlyi Mihály utca 11–15, tel: 889-3700, fax: 889-3763*. The Erzsébet is popular with both business visitors and tourists because it is centrally located and soundproofed. It is well-respected, fairly modern, mid-range and comfortable. Rooms are well equipped. 123 rooms.

Four Seasons Gresham Palace €€€€€ *V Roosevelt tér 5–6, tel: 268-6000, fax: 268-5000, <www.fourseasons.com/budapest>*. The restored Gresham Assurance Company's neo-classical palace, built 1904–6, re-opened in June 2004 as a Four Seasons Hotel. Facilities are excellent and there are specially adapted rooms for visitors with disabilities. 179 rooms.

Gold Hotel Panzió € *XIV Pándorfalu utca 15 (off Ungvár utca), tel: 252-0470, fax: 222-6982, <www.goldhotel.hu>.* A friendly suburban guesthouse. Access is easy and quick, with trolley-buses and buses stopping almost at the door, connecting to Mexikói út, City Park or Dohány utca. Rooms are simple, clean and comfortable with en-suite shower rooms. Hearty breakfast buffet. 24 rooms.

Hotel Stadion €€ *XIV Ifjúság utca 1–3, tel: 889-5200, fax: 889-5252, <www.danubiusgroup.com/stadion>.* A 1980s tower block that has been well refurbished recently. It's situated near the metro (Stadionok) and the ultra-modern sports stadium, so it's convenient for sport and pop music events. Has a fitness centre, pool, bowling alley and conference facilities. Wheelchair access. 377 rooms.

InterContinental €€€€€ *V Apáczai Csere János utca 12–14, tel: 327-6333, fax: 327-6355* Situated next to the Chain Bridge with views of the river and Buda. The facilities are top class, and the service is excellent. Convenient for business travellers as it has high-speed internet access and a business centre. Also fitness centre and pool. The Corso Restaurant has a terrace alongside the Corso, the pedestrian walkway beside the river, so guests can enjoy the view as they dine on food with Asian, Mediterranean and Hungarian influences. Two rooms have facilities for people with disabilities; one is said to be 'completely accessible'. 398 rooms.

Kempinski Hotel Corvinus €€€€€ *V Erzsébet tér 7–8, tel: 429-3777, fax: 429-4777, <www.kempinski-budapest.com>.* Architecturally striking building with a great sense of style, elegance and flair, and luxurious rooms and suites. There's an informal bistro and the respected Ristorante Giardino, decorated in Mediterranean colours and serving perfectly cooked and presented Italian cuisine. Facilities include a business centre, indoor swimming pool, fitness centre, boutiques, etc. Wheelchair access. 369 rooms.

Liget €€ *VI Dózsa György út 106, tel: 269-5300, fax: 269-5329, <www.taverna.hu>.* A modern hotel beside City Park, near Heroes' Square and the Széchenyi baths. Fully air-conditioned and with five rooms specially furnished for guests with allergies. 139 rooms.

Le Meridien Budapest €€€€€ *V Erzsébet tér 9–10, tel: 429-5500, fax: 429-5555, <www.lemeridien.com>.* The former Adria Palace, once an insurance company building, has been reborn as Le Meridien. There are seven grades of luxurious rooms and suites, all handsomely furnished. Public rooms glitter with chandeliers. The restaurant, Le Bourbon, serves food fit for a king under a regal art deco glass dome. Facilities are excellent: business centre, swimming pool, fitness centre and tennis courts. Wheelchair access. 218 rooms.

Sofitel Budapest €€€€€ *V Roosevelt tér 2, tel: 266-1234, fax 266-9101, <www.sofitel.com>.* City centre luxury hotel with views over the Danube. One of the hotel bars, called The Bridge, overlooks Chain Bridge, which is illuminated at night. The most striking feature is the atrium, which is an impressive eight floors high, decorated with palms, greenery and even a plane. The rooms are large and comfortable, and the facilities first-class, with high-tech equipment. There are also facilities for people with disabilities. 351 rooms.

Starlight Suiten €€€ *V Mérleg utca 6, tel: 484-3700, fax: 484-3711, <www.starlighthotels.com>.* This stylish, mid-size, modern apartment hotel is located conveniently close to Roosevelt tér and the Chain Bridge. Suites consist of a living room, bedroom, bathroom, and work and dressing areas. They are well equipped with microwaves and cable televisions. There's a sauna, fitness centre and cafe. 54 rooms.

Taverna €€€ *V Váci utca 20, tel: 485-3100, fax: 485-3111, <www.hoteltaverna.hu>.* Central location near Gerbeaud, the Danube and the Chain Bridge on pedestrianised Váci utca. The rooms are all generously sized and tastefully furnished. The hotel is also the site of Gambrinus, a restaurant with such splendid chefs that it has been numbered in the Hungarian top 10 every year since 1994. It's the official caterer to Parliament and therefore caters for visiting dignitaries. You can have a taste, without it costing you too much, as the Zsolnay Café brunch is prepared by Gambrinus chefs. 227 rooms.

Recommended Restaurants

The Budapest dining scene has improved dramatically in recent years, and diners now have a wider choice of cuisines and types of restaurants to eat in than ever before, including Korean, Greek, vegetarian, Mexican, Middle Eastern, Russian, Japanese, Indian and, of course, Hungarian.

Book ahead wherever possible, especially at top-tier restaurants. Many restaurants stay open throughout the afternoon. The only time when restaurants are likely to be closed is Sunday night.

All the restaurants listed in this section accept major credit cards except where noted. In Hungary, menu prices generally do not include service. However, check your bill, as some restaurants automatically add a 10 percent gratuity.

The following guidelines denote the average cost of a three-course meal for two, excluding wine and service:

€€€€	over HUF 20,000
€€€	HUF 10,000–20,000
€€	HUF 5,000–10,000
€	below HUF 5,000

BUDA AND ÓBUDA

Belgien Brasserie €–€€ *I Bem rakpart 12, tel: 201-5082.* Very laid-back and noted mainly for a fine selection of Belgian beers, but the brasserie also serves good food at keen prices. It's a great place for *moules–frites*, but there are other well-cooked and affordable dishes on the menu. It faces the Danube on the Buda side.

Fekete Holló €€€–€€€€ *I Országház utca 10, tel: 356-2367.* Set on a relatively quiet part of this popular street, the Black Raven has a small, cheerful, outdoor terrace and an attractive 18th-century dining room. Try the pancakes with caviar followed by roast wild boar – delicious.

Hemingway €€–€€€ *XI Kosztolányi Dezső tér 2, tel: 381-0522*. The proprietor is an Ernest Hemingway fan, and the décor evokes the famed writer's world. Menu is seasonal and innovative and, of course, swordfish is available. Located by Feneketlen tó (meaning bottomless lake) in a pleasant park near Móricz Zsigmond Körtér. There's a huge choice of teas, coffees and cigars on offer, and music, too.

Kéhli €€€ *III Mókus utca 22, tel: 250-4241*. Kéhli is a family-owned local tavern once the haunt of author Gyula Krúdy (1877–1933). The marrow-bone hotpot relished by Krúdy is still on the menu, which also offers Hungarian and international cuisine. Top your meal with a Transylvanian Golden Galushka pastry. Lovely summer courtyard and appropriate music.

Király Étterem €€€€ *I Táncsics Mihály utca 25, tel: 212-9891*. Good Hungarian food on Castle Hill. Stuffed meat pancakes, steaks, game, venison and good puddings – the chestnut strudel and apricot ice cream are memorable. The restaurant is circular, under a fine stained-glass dome, entertainment is gypsy music and operetta.

Mágnáskert €€€ *II Csatárka út 58, tel: 325-9967*. The restaurant is in Rózsadomb, a favoured residential district. The menu is extensive, offering traditional Hungarian dishes; game, fish and salads. They do set menus for HUF7,700 – but that's for eight courses. For the health-conscious, there's vanilla-swirl blackcurrant pudding, which is sugar-free and low-calorie.

Marxim € *II Kisrókus utca 23, tel: 316-0231*. Appropriately – given its name – this place is located near Moszkva tér. Workers of the world unite for pizza served with panache. The menu shows considerable black humour, although Gulagpizza is said to be more nourishing than it sounds. The décor is propaganda of the past and the music is loud.

Náncsi Néni Vendéglője €€–€€€ *II Ördögárok utca 80, tel: 379-2742*. A traditional restaurant with garlic and paprika dangling from the ceiling and gingham cloths and fresh bread on the tables. Pickles on the shelves can be purchased and there's a garden, so it is popular with families. Auntie Neni's home cooking is traditional, rustic Hungarian fare and it comes in heaped helpings. There's plenty of meat and fish too. The restaurant is in the Buda Hills, near the Hüvösvölgy terminal of the Children's Railway.

Tabáni Kakas €€ *I Attila út 27, tel: 357-7165.* Poultry is the speciality at this old neighbourhood favourite behind Castle Hill. Other dishes include steak tartare and crispy fried goose leg with red cabbage and mash. Peaceful atmosphere and piano music.

Vadrózsa Restaurant €€–€€€ *II Pentelei Molnár utca 15, tel: 326-5817.* The long-established restaurant is situated in a small baroque villa in Rózsadomb. Candlelight and soft piano music make it a choice spot for a romantic dinner. There's also a garden for al-fresco dining. The menu is traditional Hungarian.

PEST

Articsóka €€€ *VI Zichy Jeno utca 17, tel: 302-7757.* A few blocks from the Opera House, a large, airy and cheerful Mediterranean restaurant, the name of which means Artichoke. Serves simple Greek, Spanish and Italian fare, with occasional Hungarian dishes mixed in. There's a nice terrace and a lively crowd, many of whom spill into the restaurant from the performance space at the back.

Baraka €€–€€€ *V Magyar utca 12–14, tel: 483-1355.* Baraka is chic but understated. The cuisine is French- and Asian-influenced. The menu is short – wild duck with mango or ginger and apple soy sauce, boneless lamb and morels, and a perfect parfait with raspberry coulis. Buffet lunch HUF 1,400. Good wines by the glass.

Belcanto €€€ *VI Dalszínház utca 8, tel: 269-2786.* This place is located near the Opera, which is appropriate because Belcanto is noted for singing waiters. Don't worry, though, since the service is very good, and the catering is high-class: pasta and seafood feature. Eat-as-much-as-you-like buffet breakfast.

Café Kör €€ *V Sas utca 17, tel: 311-0053.* Near Deák tér, Café Kör offers clean white tablecloths, friendly service and reasonable prices. It is popular and you need to book for peak times. Goose-liver paté, spit roast, mixed grill, duck and some fine puddings ensure return visits. They have special menus each day. Small portions available for about 70 percent of full price. No credit cards.

Centrál Kávéház €–€€ *V Károlyi Mihály utca 9, tel: 266-2110*. This legendary café first opened in 1887 and reopened recently after nearly a half century's dormancy. Great for a good, affordable meal any time of day: soups, salads, sandwiches and more elaborate meals, and a wide selection of cakes and pies for dessert.

Cyrano €€€ *V Kristóf tér 7–8, tel: 266-3096*. This funky, chic restaurant is right at the centre of things near Váci utca, so book a table outside and watch the world go by. Menu is French/Mediterranean-inspired but with some traditional Hungarian touches. Inside, wrought-iron features in the décor, and the chandelier is from the Depardieu film of *Cyrano De Bergerac*.

Fatál €€–€€€ *V Váci utca 67, tel: 266-2607*. The exterior offers little clue as to what Fatál might offer and the name sounds a bit dubious, but it means 'wooden platter' in Hungarian, and the platters come heaped with Hungarian food, mostly quite meaty. Clientele are mainly tourists, but the food is good and the prices modest for Váci utca.

Fészek Klub €€ *VII Kertész utca 36, tel: 322-6043*. Serving an encyclopaedic menu of genuine Hungarian home-cooking in a pretty, charmingly dilapidated garden courtyard and frequented by a hip crowd. Try the Reform *bárány* (roast lamb), ragout of wild boar, game or freshwater fish dishes. Offers a set menu for HUF 1,500.

Főzelékfaló € *V Nagymező utca 18, tel: 302-3856*. Főzelék is a Hungarian thing – if it's too thin to be stew and too thick to be soup and has more or less the consistency of baby food, it's probably *főzelék*. The dish is made of vegetables such as lentils, peas, potatoes, cucumbers, green pumpkin, etc, which are thoroughly stewed before sour cream and flour are added. Devotees like a sausage or a fried egg floating on the *főzelék*. Főzelékfaló is a small, self-service place, and is usually crowded. It also serves salads.

Gerbeaud €€€ *V Vörösmarty tér 7, tel: 429-9000*. Established in 1858, the cafe is legendary. Chandeliers, marble tables and lavish décor retain the spirit of that age. Gerbeaud is renowned for cakes and cappuccino but it is far more than that. The **Lions Fountain Restaurant** (entrance on Harmincad utca) offers fine food in a romantic setting; and the bustling **Sörház** (Gerbeaud Pub) in the basement is an old-fashioned beer cellar that brews its own beer. There are also concerts in the atrium.

Gundel €€€€ *XIV Állatkerti út 2, tel: 468-4040*. Hungary's most famous and beautiful restaurant, founded in 1894, Gundel is a byword for Hungarian haute cuisine, and remains the haunt of the élite. The art nouveau décor and atmosphere have been maintained but the menu is up to date, featuring international as well as Hungarian gourmet delights, such as *fogas* (pike-perch). Be sure to save room for the famous *palacsinta* – pancakes stuffed with rum, raisins, lemon rind and walnuts, served with chocolate sauce. It isn't cheap, but the set business lunches and the Sunday brunch – all you can eat for HUF4,900 – are very reasonable. It's formal, so jackets are required for men, relatively smart dress for women, and you need to make a reservation.

Kárpátia €€–€€€ *V Ferenciek tere 7–8, tel: 317-3596*. A place that simply must be experienced. Built in 1877, with an amazing, gilded interior, this is a heritage site. The Gothic arches and walls were painted in the 1920s with scenes of the resistance to the Ottomans. The brasserie has stained glass and the courtyard has gypsy music. Transylvanian and Hungarian cuisine, goose, venison and Balaton pike-perch. The sweets are delicious: strudels and bitter-sweet orange jelly on ginger. High-quality local wines. For all this, and the central location, it's a bargain.

Marlene €€ *V Sörház utca 4, tel: 266-6676*. Newly opened restaurant and café with portraits of the iconic star. The food is innovative – start with cranberry soup or vine leaves filled with spicy goat cheese, go on to duck breast with Campari and orange sauce, or peppered catfish with garlic and brown butter, and if you've still got room for more, end with Bavarian strawberries.

Marquis de Salade €–€€ *VI Hajós utca 43, tel: 302-4086.* The proprietor is Azerbaijani and the menu is both Azerbaijani and eclectic: curry, Chinese, Italian, Bangladeshi and more, so there's an exceptional range of dishes on offer, served in generous portions. The décor is cool and white, and there are interesting tablecloths and tapestries for sale.

Mátyás Pince €€€ *V Március 15 tér 7, tel: 318-1693.* This is one of Pest's most popular tourist spots, deservedly so as it serves good, traditional Hungarian dishes, imaginatively adapted, in an atmospheric turn-of-the-20th-century cellar setting. Anyone with a healthy appetite should try the King Mátyás Platter. To round out the experience, there's gypsy music while you eat.

Múzeum Kávéház €–€€ *VI Múzeum körút 12, tel: 338-4221.* An excellent place for a meal before or after visiting the huge and potentially exhausting National Museum next door. This is a long-established classic that continues to present old Hungarian favourites, mostly featuring meat and fish. Such dishes as veal paprika, pike-perch and smoked trout are perfectly suited to the handsome Old World dining room.

Nosztalgia €€€ *V Október 6 utca 5, tel: 317-2987.* The nostalgia of the name is for the elegance of the Austro-Hungarian Empire, so there are plenty of marble columns and portraits of Empress Sissi. It evokes the good old days and the food is old-fashioned, too, although the recipes have been tweaked for today's preferences. There is brazed goose leg in garlic, but pasta and some other non-Hungarian dishes, too – all are excellent. There's music in the early evening and dancing from 10pm.

Piknik Sandwich Bar € *V Haris Köz 1, tel: 318-3334.* This is a great place for nourishing snacks, including nice, fresh open *szendvics*, cold drinks and coffee, served outdoors under shady umbrellas in the summer.

Robinson €€€ *XIV Városligeti tó (island in City Park lake), tel: 422-0222.* Appropriately, Robinson restaurant sits Crusoe-like on its own little island in the lake overlooking City Park and is perfect for outdoor eating. Excellent Hungarian and international cuisine in the restaurant, and lighter meals served in the cafe and grill (open April to September). Latin music.

Sir Lancelot €€–€€€ *Podmaniczky utca 14 (near Nyugati railway station), tel: 302-4456.* Huge portions served on wooden platters but without cutlery. Very kitsch, with waiters dressed in period costume and accompanied by appropriate music. Reservations essential.

Százéves Étterem €€€€ *V Pesti Barnabás utca 2, tel: 318-3608.* This elegant establishment, one of Budapest's oldest restaurants, is still going strong. The menu consists of new dishes created from long-neglected traditional recipes. Renowned for its game (try venison with cranberry sauce) and dishes such as tenderloin in Bull's Blood wine. Excellent wine list. Summer terrace and gypsy music.

Tom-George Restaurant and Lounge €€€ *V Október 6 utca 8, tel: 266-3525.* Newish and considered among the best in Budapest, Tom-George is located near the basilica and has a smart, design-conscious interior. The menu is a pleasing mixture of contemporary Hungarian and international and fusion cuisine. Sushi is also served, and splendid warm chocolate cake, too.

Vörös és Fehér €€–€€€ *VI Andrássy út 41, tel: 413-1545.* This is a wine bar with a massive wine list, including a dozen or more by the glass, that change weekly. Good for snacks or main meals, and you can choose from a daily list of international and Hungarian specials and a nice selection of tapas and soups. The name means 'Red and White'.

Wabisabi Reform Étterem €€ *XIII Visegrádi utca 2, tel: 412-0427.* The Wabisabi has made a name for itself as an organic, vegan restaurant, with something of a Japanese tea house feel to it. There's low seating, on Japanese-style pillows, and Zen is the order of the day. The food is healthy, with special Oriental dishes. The music is chilled-out and, as there are more than 30 kinds of tea on offer, it's a very calming experience.

INDEX